Malpractice
in Psychology

Malpractice in Psychology

A Practical Resource for Clinicians

David L. Shapiro and
Steven R. Smith

American Psychological Association • Washington, DC

Published by
American Psychological Association
750 First Street, NE
Washington, DC 20002
www.apa.org

To order
APA Order Department
P.O. Box 92984
Washington, DC 20090-2984
Tel: (800) 374-2721; Direct: (202) 336-5510
Fax: (202) 336-5502; TDD/TTY: (202) 336-6123
Online: www.apa.org/pubs/books
E-mail: order@apa.org

In the U.K., Europe, Africa, and the Middle East, copies may be ordered from
American Psychological Association
3 Henrietta Street
Covent Garden, London
WC2E 8LU England

Typeset in Minion by Circle Graphics, Inc., Columbia, MD

Printer: Maple-Vail Book Manufacturing Group, York, PA
Cover Designer: Mercury Publishing Services, Rockville, MD

The opinions and statements published are the responsibility of the authors, and such opinions and statements do not necessarily represent the policies of the American Psychological Association.

Library of Congress Cataloging-in-Publication Data

Shapiro, David L.
  Malpractice in psychology : a practical resource for clinicians / David L. Shapiro and Steven R. Smith.
    p. cm.
  ISBN-13: 978-1-4338-0895-1
  ISBN-10: 1-4338-0895-1
  1. Psychologists—Malpractice—United States. 2. Psychotherapists—Malpractice—United States. I. Smith, Steven R., 1946- II. Title.

  KF2910.P753S42 2011
  346.7303'3—dc22   2010053283

British Library Cataloguing-in-Publication Data
A CIP record is available from the British Library.

Printed in the United States of America
First Edition

DOI: 10.1037/12320-000

To Lenore
—*David L. Shapiro*

To Lera
—*Steven R. Smith*

Contents

Acknowledgments

We are most grateful to our colleagues who contributed to this book by way of reviews, suggestions, and creativity. Bob Bohrer, Steven Ciceron, Eric Drogin, Bill Lynch, Alan Nessman, Don Shapiro, and Lera Smith made many helpful comments and corrections. Megan Chambers and Scott McClain provided valuable research assistance. Shevree Galati, Marilyn Jordan, and Debbie Wilson took great care of the manuscript. The editors at the American Psychological Association deserve an award for their patience and assistance throughout the process of completing the book.

We are also indebted to the wonderful librarians who (with efficiency and good humor) were able to help us find a variety of materials from both professions. There is a considerable body of excellent work analyzing the many aspects of malpractice law and ethical considerations. We are especially thankful to the authors of these articles and books—many of whom are included in the references of this book. Of course, any errors that remain despite these efforts are solely the responsibility (malpractice?) of the authors.

In a sense, our families were responsible for this book. David notes that both of his parents were attorneys but neither of them wanted him to be a practicing attorney:

> My father wanted me to be a rabbi, because he and I loved to debate arcane (and often irrelevant) issues from the Scriptures. My mother wanted me to be a law professor, so here I am a forensic psychologist writing about the implications of malpractice law for psychologists. So, first and foremost, thanks to my parents.

Steve's experience was similar in that debates with his father over arcane issues were frequent. More recently, his family has been "always helpful and patient as a seemingly unending series of books, reprints, drafts and redrafts were dragged through most rooms of our house."

We also thank the many dedicated professionals who have devoted their careers to improving the psychological and legal professions. Malpractice inevitably focuses primarily on bad practice. Fortunately, some of the best members of our professions have studied malpractice and ethics, thereby improving the professions and the quality of services we provide to our clients. Our colleagues on various ethics and other professional committees have also helped sharpen our ability to analyze tricky ethical and professional issues. To these professionals we extend our profound thanks and respect. We hope this book makes a small contribution to that honorable tradition.

Most important, we thank our wives, Lenore Walker and Lera Smith, who have profoundly influenced our ideas. Both are steady influences, always gently but forcefully challenging us to explore our assertions and make our writing clearer and more readable.

Malpractice
in Psychology

Introduction

Malpractice liability is a fact of modern professional life for psychologists. There is a monetary threat, of course, but malpractice is also a threat to the reputation of therapists. Concern about malpractice, ignited by horror stories of lawsuits, can lead to unnecessarily cautious practice ("defensive medicine"; Hedges, 2007; Tellefsen, 2009). Fortunately, therapists can do something about malpractice.

At professional seminars we are frequently asked "How can I keep from getting sued?" The answer is: You cannot. Psychologists can, however, minimize the risk of being sued *successfully* and can reduce the likelihood of facing even an unfounded malpractice claim (Bennett et al., 2006).

To deal effectively with the threat of malpractice, psychologists must first understand the legal bases for liability (described in Chapters 1 and 2) and then specific areas and situations that give rise to practice liability (addressed in Chapters 3–8). In this book we suggest ways in which psychologists can avoid malpractice claims (some practical suggestions are made in Chapter 9 and at the conclusion of most of the other chapters).

SHOULD PSYCHOLOGISTS BE CONCERNED ABOUT MALPRACTICE?

To the question of whether psychologists should be concerned about malpractice, we firmly answer "No and yes": "no" because, as readers will see, malpractice claims in psychology are relatively unusual, at least compared with those in many other health care professions, and "yes" because malpractice liability is very real and, though still rare, probably increasing for psychologists. Psychologists should take into account professional liability risks in establishing practice routines and in all practice areas. It is easy to do this, and doing so can simultaneously reduce the risk of a claim, improve relationships with clients, and provide greater professional peace of mind (Sales, Miller, & Hall, 2005).

Informed consent is an example of how a legal doctrine can improve professional practice. Bennett et al. (2006) noted that the likelihood of malpractice lawsuits decreased when psychologists carefully explained procedures to clients and encouraged them to express questions and concerns. Clients who become involved in litigation against their psychologists often state that the doctor had not provided sufficient information, had not respected their opinions or points of view, or had withheld important information (Bennett, Bryant, VandenBos, & Greenwood, 1990). Bennett et al. also suggested that psychologists spend more time on informed consent and involve the clients more fully in the decision-making process.

WHAT MALPRACTICE REALLY IS

Put informally, *malpractice liability* is bad professional practice that results in injury. Put more precisely, psychologists are subject to malpractice liability when their practice falls below the standard of reasonable care of the profession and, as a direct result, someone is injured (S. R. Smith, 1996). *Reasonable practice* is generally defined by the profession itself—by what professionals generally do under the circumstances and the basic norms of the profession (Crawford, 1994). Ethics and malpractice often address the same concerns of unprofessional conduct, which is why we refer frequently to professional ethical standards in this book. (Bersoff, 2008).

The American Psychological Association (APA, 2010), National Association of Social Workers (2008), Canadian Psychological Association (2000), American Association of Marriage and Family Therapists (2001), and American Psychiatric Association (2009) each have their own code of ethics, but they share many core values. As an example, the APA (2010) "Ethical Principles of Psychologists and Code of Conduct" (http://www.apa.org/ethics/code/index.aspx) consists of five broad principles, which are aspirational in nature, and 10 enforceable standards. Violation of the latter may, under some circumstances, lead to a variety of sanctions being imposed on the psychologist.

A violation of ethics codes and an example of malpractice, at the extreme, is sexual misconduct, which is clearly improper and unethical conduct and a common complaint in malpractice cases (B. Caudill, 2001; Roberts, Monferrari, & Yeager, 2008). It naturally gives rise to liability. Another example of failure to meet professional standards is breach of confidentiality. Confidentiality is frequently cited by psychologists as an important, perhaps essential, part of therapy. For that reason it is a clear professional obligation, the breach of which can be malpractice.

Practicing outside the bounds of one's competence is not acceptable professional practice and can lead to malpractice liability (S. R. Smith, 2000). The APA Ethics Code defines *competence* as having sufficient knowledge, education, training, supervision, and professional experience to practice in a particular area. The psychologist who perceives her- or himself as a "jack of all trades," willing to undertake any kind of evaluation or treatment, is violating professional norms and inviting litigation.

In the typical malpractice case, the psychologist has breached an obligation to a client. In a few instances, psychologists have legal obligations to a third party who is not a client. We discuss in Chapter 6 the obligation to warn or protect third parties from dangerous clients (e.g., *Tarasoff v. Regents of the University of California, 1974*).

Psychologists have many legal defenses against claims of malpractice. In the majority of health care cases that go to trial, these defenses are successful and there is no liability (Kohn, Corrigan, & Donaldson, 2000). Specific defenses vary depending on the nature of the malpractice claim, and we note various defenses throughout this book.

But malpractice claims have increased

TRENDS IN MALPRACTICE LITIGATION

Although malpractice claims against psychologists are relatively infrequent compared with those against practitioners of such medical specialties as neurosurgery and obstetrics, there has been an increase in these claims. During the early years in which malpractice insurance was offered to psychologists (1973–1975), there were 37 claims against psychologists (Cohen, 1979). The APA Insurance Trust has offered professional liability insurance to APA members since 1976. From 1976 to 1989, 1,416 claims were filed against psychologists insured by the Trust. An average of 125 claims were reported each year (Bennett et al.,1990). Interestingly, in these early years a number of claims revolved around fee disputes, not true malpractice claims. Sexual impropriety was the second most frequent complaint. Nevertheless, the complaints filed were still relatively rare (Cohen, 1979).

By 1980, claims paid by the APA Insurance Trust were over $400,000 (S. R. Smith, 1991, p. 212). Current figures suggest that there has been some increase, but nowhere as dramatic as the public misperception of a malpractice crisis would suggest. In 2005–2006, the Trust paid approximately $750,000 to defend malpractice claims (G. Koocher, personal communication, July 2009). These cases involved suicides, boundary violations (nonsexual), sexual misconduct, billing improprieties, and one homicide.

An informal survey of colleagues suggests that in clinical psychology, the average annual fee for malpractice insurance has jumped by at least a factor of 15 in the past 30 years; that is, a mental health professional in solo practice who paid $100 annually in 1980 now pays at least $1,500 in an annual malpractice premium. Individuals in group practices or who employ other psychologists pay even higher rates.

The accuracy of these data is complicated by several difficulties in finding complete claims records. There are multiple insurance carriers, and some do not provide clear claims information. It is especially difficult to obtain reliable data on such claims as sexual misconduct. Also, some practitioners work for state and federal agencies that may be self-insured (Bennett et al., 2006). In addition, it is often difficult to delineate these categories precisely and obtain exact percentages for each type of malpractice case. The premiums psychologists pay, of course, reflect the cost of insurance companies defending not only legitimate claims but also totally spurious ones.

Statistics from the APA Insurance Trust provide insight into the areas most likely to give rise to a malpractice claim. Bennett et al. (2006) presented data indicating that the most common malpractice complaints are

- ineffective treatment, failure to consult and/or refer—29%;
- negligent diagnosis—16%;
- child custody evaluations—10%;
- sexual misconduct—9%;
- breach of confidentiality—8%;
- suicide—4%; and
- inadequate supervision—3%.

Other allegations included conflicts of interest, defamation, abandonment, abuse, and discrimination.

CAN PSYCHOLOGISTS AVOID MALPRACTICE?

If psychologists would refrain from boundary violations, use well-validated assessment instruments appropriate for the case at issue, practice only within the limits of their competence, obtain informed consent to all procedures, and use appropriate fee collection policies they could significantly reduce the rate of successful malpractice actions against their profession. There is no mystery in this formulation. It is simply a statement of good professional practice.

Even better than winning a malpractice case is not having a lawsuit filed for malpractice in the first place. Claims of malpractice that are without merit can disrupt and harm a psychologist. Throughout this book we suggest ways that psychologists can reduce the possibility of being sued, even in those instances where such a claim is unjustified.

Psychologists are, to some degree, protected against malpractice claims because even when harm has been done, clients may be reluctant to file a claim against a psychologist. "In the past, mental health practitioners have been protected from liability by a variety of legal rules and the stigma

Reasons for rarity of malpractice claims

associated with being a mental patient" (S. R. Smith, 1991, p. 211). Clients who initiate cases cast their mental condition into the public arena. The close relationship between a client and a therapist also has fostered reluctance to file professional liability suits. The quality of the therapist–client relationship has a great deal to do with whether a suit is filed: The stronger the professional relationship, the less likely the practitioner is to be sued (Bennett et al., 2006; S. R. Smith, 1991). As readers will see, psychologists can do many things to reduce the risk that harm to a client or third party will lead to a successful malpractice claim.

LAWS THAT APPLY TO MALPRACTICE

Most malpractice cases are governed by state law. States generally supply rules governing professional liability, the licensing of professionals, and the legal duties of professionals. Liability rules as well as rules of procedure and evidence are ordinarily state based. Therefore, most malpractice cases are tried in state court, with state laws being applied. One consequence of the importance of state law is that the rules and procedures concerning malpractice claims and liability in general may vary from one state to another. Fortunately, these variations in state law tend to be in the details as opposed to the broad principles, so it is possible to make generalizations about malpractice claims for most states. Nonetheless, readers are encouraged to check their own state laws.

Federal law and federal courts do play a role in mental health law. For example, the Health Insurance Portability and Accountability Act of 1996 (HIPAA) and the Americans with Disabilities Act of 1990 (ADA) create federal rights that may subject therapists to liability.

A NOTE ON CASES

Many cases are used as examples throughout this book. With few exceptions, we use these cases for illustrative purposes rather than to state a uniformly accepted principle of law. Many are officially reported cases that have formal citations (most cases are also online). In other instances, we describe cases without citation that come from the experience of the authors and are not officially reported. The names are withheld for privacy reasons. In some instances these unofficial cases are composites of several cases.

ORGANIZATION OF THIS BOOK

The purpose of this book is to help psychologists understand the legal bases of liability and the reality of malpractice (as opposed to urban legends, and there are many of those), and to help them take reasonable steps to limit the risk of malpractice claims. We first deal with the theory and general legal principles of malpractice and then translate those principles into practical ways of avoiding the risk and the unnecessary concerns about professional liability.

In the first two chapters, we provide an overview of the law of professional liability, in particular negligence. The next several chapters deal with professional liability and informed consent, confidentiality, diagnosis and treatment, and violence. In a separate chapter, we consider a variety of other areas of practice that give rise to liability. In the last two chapters, we review the trial process and risk management strategies. Because avoiding claims and liability is a focus of this book, most chapters include practical suggestions to assist psychologists in that goal.

Malpractice claims are a risk of professional practice. This is a risk, however, that psychologists can manage and minimize.

1

Tort Liability Basics

The word *malpractice* is usually used to mean "liability arising out of professional practice." It is most commonly a tort action against a professional. A *tort* is a noncontractual civil harm. A *torts case* (as opposed to a criminal case) is one in which an injured person seeks damages on the basis of a claim that someone else wrongfully caused harm. In the law, a "person" may be an individual or a legal entity such as a corporation, partnership, or estate. When a large group of individuals sues collectively over a similar issue, it may result in what is termed a *class action*.

There are two general goals of the tort system. The first is to provide money to remedy or pay for the harm caused by another's wrongful conduct; this is known as *compensation*. The second goal, *deterrence*, seeks to reduce bad conduct by penalizing undesirable or harmful conduct that causes injury.

The three broad categories of torts are (a) intentional torts, (b) negligence, and (c) strict liability. It is generally said in the law that, unlike contractual liability, tort duties are imposed by society instead of voluntarily assumed through a contract. As a general matter, however, tort duties arise from the voluntary undertaking of activities or roles. For example, legal duties are imposed by society on someone who drives a car or practices psychology, but a person voluntarily becomes a driver or practices psychology.

In torts a private party seeks monetary damages, whereas in criminal law the government seeks to punish a wrongdoer. The process and concepts used in a criminal case are substantially different from those in a torts case. One notable example is the level of proof required. Whereas the prosecution in a criminal case must prove its case "beyond a reasonable doubt"—a very high standard of proof—in most torts cases the plaintiff must prove liability by a "preponderance of the evidence" (i.e., that it is more likely than not) that the defendant wrongfully caused harm to the plaintiff. The same conduct can give rise to more than one tort, as well as to both tort and criminal liability; that is, a therapist may be convicted of a crime, and be liable in malpractice, for the same misconduct. If a therapist has sexual relations with a client in a state where that is illegal, for example, the state may prosecute the therapist, and the client may also sue for damages (Strasburger, Jorgenson, & Randles, 2008). The therapist may also be subject to licensure discipline.

Professional liability can be based on a number of legal doctrines, but it is most commonly based on the concept of negligence. In *negligence cases*, the plaintiff will allege that the defendant breached a duty of care and, as a result, the plaintiff suffered harm.

In recent years, in some states, *malpractice* has taken on a special meaning as a result of tort reform (McClellan, 2006). Some state legislatures have passed statutes that create special rules for malpractice cases, including limitations on certain types of damages. Their applicability to mental health professionals varies among states and even according to the type of licensing and functions of the professional (*Karasek v. LaJoie*, 1998).

Tort cases are most commonly (but not always) filed in state courts. State law and state court procedures apply in these cases. However, several federal laws can affect the practice of psychology and impose liability. In addition, some tort cases are tried in federal courts because the plaintiff and defendant are citizens of different states.

Malpractice and other civil lawsuits seldom go to trial (Bogie & Marine, 2009). The vast majority, over 90%, of civil lawsuits are settled before trial

Most suits don't go to trial

or before a judgment is final (Matthews, 2003). Settlements often occur after many months of discovery (during which each side seeks relevant information from the other and from expert witnesses) and preliminary wrangling. In addition, insurance can play a significant role in this process. We discuss the trial and settlement process in the last two chapters of this book.

NEGLIGENCE

The overwhelming majority of malpractice cases are based on the tort of negligence. (The term *negligence* can be a bit confusing because it refers not only to a kind of carelessness but also to a specific tort.) The four basic elements of the tort of negligence, whether driving a car or practicing psychology, are (a) duty, (b) breach of duty, (c) causation, and (d) injury. A broad statement of the *duty of care* is that one is obligated to act as a reasonably careful person would under the same circumstances. The driver of a car, for example, must act as a "reasonably prudent" driver would considering the road conditions. When the driver is not acting reasonably (e.g., is speeding), the driver has breached the duty of care and is said to be *negligent*. If that negligence does not harm anyone else, then there is no civil liability (the driver may, however, face criminal charges). If, however, the driving causes injury to someone else (e.g., because of excessive speed the driver hits another car), then there will be *liability*. The liability is not a reflection on or related to the general driving skills of the negligent driver (known as the *tortfeasor*). The driver may be widely known as an outstanding and very careful motorist. The question is whether, in this instance, the driver breached the standard of care.

Similar concepts apply in malpractice or professional liability cases based on negligence. Mental health practitioners are subject to liability for negligence when their practice deviates from professionally accepted standards and a client (or, in some cases, a third party) is harmed as a result. A psychologist, of course, is held not to the standard of reasonable care of a prudent person but rather to the standard of care of a reasonably prudent psychologist operating under the same or similar circumstances. Most often this is determined by what professionals actually do under these circumstances (Ash, 2010). The apparently simple formulation of negligence (duty, breach of duty, causation, and injury) is actually quite complicated when applied to professional practice. We review these issues, as they apply to the practice of psychology, in some detail, in Chapter 2. Malpractice liability does not imply that a psychologist is generally careless, a bad psychologist, or unethical. Instead, it indicates that in this instance professional negligence caused an injury. Even the best psychologist can make a mistake that results in injury.

Negligence liability occurs only when the injuries are caused by unreasonable errors. Just as a driver who is carefully driving down the street is not negligent if he strikes someone who suddenly darts from between parked trucks, neither is a psychologist negligent for bad outcomes that occurred within the scope of reasonable professional judgment. If there is an acceptable body of literature that supports what the practitioner did, then she or he was generally not behaving unreasonably.

Bad practice, regardless of how far it deviates from acceptable standards, results in negligence liability only if the plaintiff can demonstrate that the negligence caused a legally recognizable injury. In ethics cases or cases brought before a licensing board, in general such an injury is not necessary. The factual question of causation can be a major issue in mental health malpractice cases, in part because the cause of a mental health problem can be so hard to establish.

In establishing causation, experts play an important role. They are called on to testify whether, in their professional judgment, an injury or harm occurred because of the therapist's negligence. These experts' opinions frequently are clinical judgments about which there are professional disagreements, resulting in the judge or jury having to decide the complex issue of causation.

Because the plaintiff has the burden of proving all elements of negligence, including causation, uncertainty regarding causation often benefits the defense. The problem of *hindsight bias*, of course, is that once something bad has happened it is common for jurors to presume that negligence caused the injury. We consider various aspects of negligence liability in Chapter 2 and throughout this book.

INTENTIONAL TORTS

Although negligence is the primary form of malpractice liability, *intentional torts* are sometimes the basis for liability. Intentional torts include battery, intentional infliction of emotional distress, assault, and false imprisonment. In each of these torts, the defendant or tortfeasor (person committing the tort) has deliberately done an act, without legal justification, that is likely to be harmful or offensive. For example, when one person deliberately hits another, this is *battery*. When someone acts outrageously, expecting it to cause severe distress to another, this may be *intentional infliction of emotional distress*. *Assault* may be committed by intentionally placing another in fear of an imminent battery. *False imprisonment* occurs when the defendant intends to confine someone and prevents that person from leaving a specific area (e.g., hospital, car, room).

In each of these examples, the defendant has *intentionally* invaded a legally protected interest of the plaintiff. That intent is the essential mental state underlying all intentional torts, and it separates these torts from negligence. Mere carelessness or bad judgment is not enough for an intentional tort, as it would be for negligence. Instead, in intentional torts the defendants must have actually intended to act in a manner that results in an invasion of legally protected interests, or they must have known that this invasion of interests was substantially certain to follow from their conduct.

Intentional torts can occur in mental health practice. For example, a mental health professional who slaps a client to calm the person down may have committed battery. A researcher who deliberately puts subjects through extremely stressful circumstances (e.g., falsely reporting the death of a parent) to judge their reactions to stress has probably committed an intentional infliction of emotional distress.

Even if well intentioned, a deliberate act may cause liability. A surgeon who performs unwanted surgery for the client's own good may have committed battery. Similarly, a mental health professional who locks up and holds a client for the client's own good, without legal justification, may have committed the intentional tort of false imprisonment.

Intent does not necessarily mean that one party set out to deliberately harm the other party. Instead, the tortfeasor intended a certain act and knew, or believed with a substantial certainty, that the act is not consented to, and could be offensive or could cause harm.

The possibility of an intentional tort arises when a professional knowingly misuses a therapeutic modality. Such cases could involve somatic treatments, such as electroconvulsive therapy, or medication. A physician, for instance, who prescribes electroconvulsive therapy not for therapeutic purposes but to punish an unruly client could be seen as committing an intentional tort. In a similar manner, a physician who aggressively prescribes certain medications that are known to have serious side effects merely for the convenience of keeping a client quiet, rather than for any legitimate therapeutic purpose, may be risking liability for an intentional tort.

The word *intentional* may suggest that somehow both the expert witness and the trier of fact (judge or jury) need to understand what was going through the defendant's head at the time of the tortious action. This is not so. Assessing the actual mental state of a defendant is, of course, impossible. Juries can infer, however, the necessary intent from the actions and statements of the defendant. The legal standard for an intentional tort is sometimes derived from facts that a jury would understand without the need for expert testimony. For instance, in *Hammer v. Rosen* (1960), a therapist beat one of his clients as part of the client's "therapy." The judge ruled that there was no need for expert testimony, that the very nature of the act established improper treatment and malpractice.

STRICT LIABILITY

The third major branch of torts is *strict liability*. Whereas negligence requires carelessness, and intentional torts require that the defendant intentionally invaded a legally protected interest, strict liability is imposed without any specific fault by the defendant. Strict liability is most commonly used in cases where defective products cause injury. It also appears in several areas of the law unrelated to the practice of psychology (e.g., abnormally dangerous activities, keeping wild animals). Although strict liability has become common in products liability, that trend is not making its way into services. It is unlikely that strict liability will become a form of professional liability.

One form of strict liability will be familiar to psychologists who maintain their own offices. Workers' compensation is a kind of strict liability in which compensation is awarded to an employee injured at work, even though the employer was absolutely blameless and could have done nothing to prevent the injury.

EMPLOYEE AND AGENTS

Psychologists may be liable for negligently selecting or hiring assistants and other employees. If a psychologist carelessly selects an incompetent assistant (e.g., by failing to do even minimal reference checking) who injures a client, the psychologist's negligence in hiring can result in liability. Even in the absence of negligence, however, the law imposes *vicarious liability* on employers, or *principals,* for the actions of employees or agents. Because psychologists often employ assistants, paraprofessionals, and other staff in professional practice, it is important to have some understanding of this liability. In addition, in some instances, partners (i.e., in a group practice) may give rise to vicarious liability (Morgan, Soetaert, & Heinrichs, 2008).

A professional may be civilly liable for the negligence of an employee who is working within the scope of her or his employment. Suppose, for instance, that a psychologist employs a psychometrician to score tests. If the psychometrician negligently scores a test and that faulty scoring harms a client of the psychologist, the psychologist who employs the psychometrician may be liable for the harm. This vicarious liability arises even though the employing psychologist did everything possible to avoid scoring errors.

Vicarious liability is not limited to employees. Partners are generally considered vicariously liable to clients and other third parties for each other's negligence. Thus, three psychologists in a partnership may each be responsible for the professional negligence of the other two. For this reason, many psychologists are opting to establish practices that are not organized as partnerships or unincorporated associations and instead are setting their practices up as a limited liability corporation or similar organizational structure. (For general advice on setting up a practice, see Vaughn & Gentry, 2006.)

SUPERVISION

Although vicarious liability applies to agents and employees, it does not apply to the work of independent contractors. (It is still possible, of course, for there to be negligence liability in the selection or review and supervision of independent contractors.) The essential difference between an agent and an independent contractor is the right to control and direct activities. The agent has the *right* to exercise control, and the failure to actually exercise control does not eliminate vicarious liability. In the preceding section, we offered the hypothetical example of a psychometrician employed by a psychologist. Suppose, instead, that the psychologist used a scoring service that used the psychometrician. The psychologist did not have any opportunity to control how the psychometrician worked. It is likely, in that case, that the service and the psychometrician would be independent contractors, and vicarious liability would not apply.

A psychologist's supervision of persons in training (e.g., interns) or of other psychologists creates the possibility of vicarious liability. It is clear that the failure to exercise appropriate and careful oversight of someone under supervision is negligence and can give rise to liability (Saccuzzo, 1997). Suppose, for example, a psychologist has agreed to supervise a master's level practitioner who is in quasi-independent practice but then never reviews the supervisee's records, seldom consults with the supervisee, does not hold regular sessions to review the supervisee's work, and otherwise is generally unaware of what the supervisee is doing. The supervising psychologist is risking liability for failure to engage in reasonable supervision. Indeed, in this example the supervision is essentially a sham (Recupero & Rainey, 2007). Standard 2.05 ("Delegation of Work to Others") of the American Psychological Association's (2010) "Ethical Principles of Psychologists and Code of Conduct" (http://www.apa.org/ethics/code/index.aspx) addresses issues related to supervision.

In addition to negligence due to improper supervision, however, some supervision creates a likely form of agency in which the supervisor will be liable for actions of the supervisee under agency/vicarious liability. These cases are generally fact specific, so liability will depend on the specific circumstances. As a broad principle, however, the greater the opportunities (regardless of whether they are exercised) for the supervisor to direct the work of the supervisee, the greater the potential for vicarious liability (Saccuzzo, 1997).

When supervising interns, residents, or employees, a psychologist should maintain close scrutiny over their work and be familiar with their activities. Suppose a therapist established clinics at various sites across a state and employed master's level counselors at all of the sites. On paper, he was listed as a "supervisor," but he rarely provided any face-to-face supervision. A child seen by one of the counselors experienced a psychotic break and had to be hospitalized. The supervising psychologist could be liable under the theory of vicarious liability (with the counselor as agents) or for his own negligence (carelessness in selecting and supervising the counselors).

OTHER FORMS OF PROFESSIONAL LIABILITY

Although torts are the basis for the majority of professional liability cases, liability may arise from other legal sources. Contract law, for example, may provide the legal basis for claims against psychologists. State and federal statutes are increasingly playing an important role in civil claims against psychologists. Notable examples include federal and state privacy laws, and civil rights statutes, all of which may give rise to liability (Hall & Resnick, 2008). These statutory provisions sometimes modify or even limit existing common law tort recovery (e.g., state *Tarasoff* statutes; see Chapter 6, this volume, for more details), expand on traditional malpractice concepts (e.g., federal modifications to the Health Insurance Portability and Accountability Act of 1996 regarding privacy), or create whole new areas of liability (e.g., child abuse reporting requirements). Later in this book we discuss a number of significant statutory claims.

The practice of psychology also makes professionals subject to a wide variety of business and professional laws and obligations: business association (practice structure), property (landlord–tenant), taxation, licensing, employee safety—the list seems endless. A thorough discussion of those business and professional legal obligations is beyond the scope of this book. They suggest the need, however, for psychologists to establish a continuing, preventive-law relationship with an attorney (Pope & Vasquez, 2005a), a topic we address in Chapter 9.

DAMAGES

Monetary damages are nearly always the recovery in a malpractice case in which the plaintiff (client) prevails. The general purpose of damages is, to the extent possible through money, to put the plaintiffs back in the position they would have been in had the tort not caused injury.

Compensatory Damages

Tort damages that compensate a plaintiff for the harm suffered can broadly be divided into economic and noneconomic damages. *Economic damages* include those both already incurred and anticipated future expenses for medical care, personal care, lost wages and other income, and disability or impairment (e.g., the loss of an arm).

Noneconomic damages are awarded for pain and suffering (in general, physical pain) and mental distress or suffering (e.g., anxiety, embarrassment, fright, humiliation, loss of peace of mind). Although mental distress damages are available for intentional torts (intentional infliction of emotional distress), the law traditionally (with some exceptions) has awarded mental suffering damages in negligence cases only if there is a physical injury, a physical manifestation of an emotional harm, or some other extraordinary event. Damages for mental distress, however, are common in personal injury cases that involve physical injuries. The compensation for emotional harm is especially difficult to determine or predict with any certainty (Tomlinson, 2009). Jury sympathy for an injured plaintiff probably inflates awarded damages, whereas a sympathetic defendant probably reduces them.

Some torts provide for other kinds of damages. In defamation or some privacy cases, for example, damage to reputation is compensable. Although recovery in civil actions is generally limited to a monetary award, in some special circumstances the court may issue an injunction by which it orders one of the parties to do or not do something specific (e.g., turn over records, leave a party alone).

It is common for expert witnesses to help the jury (or judge) establish a fair value of damages. Mental health experts may be able to discuss the likely future costs of therapy, for example. Rehabilitation experts may testify about the effect of an injury on the plaintiff's ability to work or study. Economic and accounting experts also are used to consider the present value of an injury or how to calculate a *structured settlement,* under which payments may be made to the defendant over time.

Punitive Damages

In a few cases, the conduct of the defendant is so outrageous that *punitive damages* are awarded. Also known as *exemplary damages,* these are seen not as compensation for a loss but as an expression of strong disapproval of the defendant's acts. These damages are added to the compensatory damages. Cases against mental health professionals that result in punitive damages usually involve some form of sexual or financial exploitation.

Nominal Damages

The plaintiff, in most lawsuits, receives damages in the amount to compensate for actual injuries. In some cases however, plaintiffs may receive a token amount (often $1). The purpose of such *nominal damages* is to indicate that the plaintiff's complaint is legitimate, even though the plaintiff has not demonstrated any actual injury. Defamation is an area in which a nominal damage may be justified (see our discussion in Chapter 3). Such damages are generally not available in negligence cases.

THE VULNERABLE CLIENT

There is a cliché in tort law that "You take your victim as you find him or her." This means that a tortfeasor is responsible for the damages to the victim of the tort even though, because of peculiarities of the victim, the harm was much greater than expected. The traditional example is the case of the "eggshell plaintiff," in which a defendant hits the plaintiff on the head (commits a battery) but because of the weakness of the plaintiff's skull causes much greater damage than would ordinarily occur. The defendant is still responsible for all of the damages. In mental health malpractice cases, the fact that negligence results in greater injury to the plaintiff than could have been expected will probably fall within this rule. The causation is not "cut off" by the weakness of the plaintiff. For example, if a therapist negligently gives a client bad advice and this causes the client, who is unusually emotionally fragile, to become extremely depressed and attempt suicide, the therapist would still be liable for the full resulting damages (Bongar, 2002).

IS MONEY ENOUGH?

Although monetary damages are the legal remedy plaintiffs seek, it is likely that money is not really the goal, or at least not the only goal, of many mental health malpractice claims. The reality is that damages awarded by courts often do not address the harm that the plaintiff feels. A sense of betrayal, lack of caring, and breach of trust cannot be addressed by monetary damages. These elements of harm can play a role in negotiating out-of-court settlements or arrangements that are meaningful to the plaintiff/client and within the professional goals of mental health practitioners.

The issues discussed in the preceding sections are important considerations that lawyers and mental health professionals should keep in mind as settlements or informal resolutions to claims are considered. The place of a genuine apology in malpractice is now being recognized (Runnels, 2009). Some clients who are injured are seeking an explanation of what happened, peace of mind, or reassurance that what happened to them will not happen to others—a kind of psychic compensation (Wexler, 2008).

TORT AND MALPRACTICE REFORM

A number of states have passed statutes changing the ordinary rules in medical malpractice cases. These reforms frequently shorten the statute of limitations or place maximum awards, or *caps*, on noneconomic damages (caps limit these damages to a specific dollar amount, e.g., $250,000) (Matthews, 2003). These statutes vary from state to state, and several state courts have declared them unconstitutional.

The purpose of such reforms is to encourage health practitioners to continue to practice in the state, reduce defensive medicine (practice aimed only at limiting the possibility of lawsuits instead of providing good care), and reduce excessive insurance premiums for some medical specialties. The objection to the cap reforms is that they remove some incentives for professionals to be especially careful to protect clients. Another objection is that these laws are fundamentally unfair because they treat plaintiffs with similar injuries differently (McClellan, 2006). For example, suppose Plaintiff A and Plaintiff B both become paraplegic through the negligence of Dr. Z, Plaintiff A because of Dr. Z's bad driving and Plaintiff B because of Dr. Z's malpractice. Their ability to recover noneconomic damages above a cap of, say, $250,000 is different. Plaintiff A could receive unlimited noneconomic damages, but for the same injuries Plaintiff B's noneconomic damages would be limited to $250,000 (Garber, Greenberg, Rhodes, Zhou, & Adams, 2009).

Some mental health practice is covered by these reform statutes, but it varies a great deal. The specific language of the statute is critical in determining what forms of mental health malpractice cases are covered by the state law and the degree to which psychologists are included. This is an area in flux, with legislatures changing the law and courts limiting or interpreting reform laws frequently (Moncrieff, 2009).

A number of efforts have been made to provide malpractice reform at the federal level. If adopted, these reforms could well have some impact on malpractice in psychology.

PRACTICAL SUGGESTIONS

1. Understand the basics of malpractice liability. Psychologists who understand the bases of malpractice claims are in a good position to know how to avoid malpractice difficulties.
2. Understand the concept of negligence. Negligence is the basis of the vast majority of malpractice claims. The traditional elements of negligence

are duty, breach of the duty, causation, and injury. Put more simply, in most situations someone is required to act with reasonable care to avoid harming others. There are specialized formulations of this for psychologists as indicated in the American Psychological Association Ethics Code.

3. Be aware of the potential for vicarious liability. It can be an important form of liability in private practice. A psychologist may be liable for the negligence of agents, employees, partners, and some individuals practicing under the psychologist's supervision.

4. New kinds of professional liability are being developed by statute and regulation by federal and state governments. Psychologists should understand these developing forms of liability.

5. A recurring theme of this book is that it is wise for psychologists to create and maintain continuing professional relationships with an attorney who can help them understand the relevant law in their states and who can help establish office procedures, records, and risk reduction programs. An attorney can also help establish proper forms, office organization, and insurance plans.

2

Negligence in Professional Practice

We noted in Chapter 1 that mental health practitioners are subject to negligence liability when their practice deviates from professionally accepted practice (the standard of care) and a client is harmed as a result. In this chapter, we look at each of the four apparently simple elements of negligence, the tort that accounts for the vast majority of malpractice actions: (a) duty, (b) breach of duty, (c) causation, and (d) damages. In practice they are not so simple.

THE STANDARD OF CARE: DUTY AND THE BREACH OF DUTY

The phrase *standard of care* is commonly used to describe the duty a professional owes to a client. This basically means doing what a reasonably careful practitioner would do under the circumstances. In the case of a specialist, the standard of care is increased to what a reasonably careful practitioner of that specialty would do under the circumstances. This means that the practitioner is being judged against prevailing professional standards (Belar & Deardorff, 2009). For instance, a psychologist whose client with borderline personality disorder has a poor outcome would be judged against standards of an average professional, not against a standard of the most outstanding, well-established practitioner.

In most cases, a therapist's legal duty of care is to the client, not to third parties or to society in general. It is therefore critical to know whether a therapy relationship exists (something we consider in detail in Chapter 3). As readers will see, the law is also now recognizing some duty to third parties when a client may harm them.

Applying the Standard of Care

The concept of a legally acceptable standard of care may seem ambiguous to psychologists. It is true that there is often no bright line that defines what is acceptable and what is not, but that often works to the advantage of the psychologist in malpractice cases.

It may be helpful to think of the standard of care as reflecting a level of practice that is acceptable within the profession itself. The negligence may be by *commission* (the therapist did something that she or he should not have done) or *omission* (the therapist failed to do something that she or he should have done). The psychologist need not have picked the "best" option for treatment; he or she needs only to have acted within the range of what a reasonable practitioner would have done under the circumstances. Bad results sometimes occur even in the absence of any negligence, so bad results alone do not prove negligence. A client may commit suicide even after receiving good care (Baerger, 2001). Furthermore, even when a psychologist makes a mistake, that is not sufficient to prove negligence; in other words, not all mistakes occur because of negligence. There are *reasonable* and *unreasonable* mistakes; a reasonable mistake is one that a careful practitioner could have made under the circumstances.

The standard of care commonly includes a range of options for treating a client. In psychology there often is not a single professionally accepted approach to treating a client's problems. Within mental health care there are often various approaches to dealing with a disorder. These are called *schools of thought* in malpractice cases. Adding the concept of school of thought to the negligence definition would make it this: "Is what the psy-

26

chologist did consistent with what a reasonable practitioner of a legitimate school of thought would have done under the circumstances?" Practitioners ordinarily are held to the professional standard of care of the school of thought to which they belong (see Standard 2.04, "Bases for Scientific and Professional Judgments," of the American Psychological Association's [APA's, 2010] "Ethical Principles of Psychologists and Code of Conduct"; http://www.apa.org/ethics/code/index.aspx). A cognitive behavioral therapist and a psychoanalytically oriented therapist would be held to the standards of their own schools of thought. Many conditions do not have good comparative data on the efficacy of various approaches, so there are many accepted positions on appropriate treatment. Courts have sometimes held religious counselors to a different standard because they endorse a school of thought that combines religion with therapy (Young & Griffith, 1999).

It is often difficult to establish a clear standard of care in the mental health disciplines. As of 1990, there were more than 200 schools of thought (S. R. Smith, 1991, p. 214) regarding mental health practice. A more recent estimate is that now there are 250 (Parry & Drogin, 2007).

A psychologist need not adhere to a single school of thought for every condition, or even for every client. Mental health professionals may adopt an eclectic approach to different conditions or different clients, but they are expected to be proficient in whatever approach they use.

The other side of the school-of-thought coin is that professionals can be held responsible for having any special skills, training, or knowledge that they claim to have. This is called *holding oneself out liability;* that is, if a therapist has claimed an expertise as a specialist—say, in child psychology—then that therapist is going to be held to the standard of an expert or specialist in child psychology, regardless of whether the therapist has such expertise. Standard 2.01 ("Boundaries of Competence") of the APA Ethics Code addresses issues related to expertise and training as they relate to competence. The public should be able to depend on the claims professionals make about their abilities, and one way the law enforces this is to hold professionals to an especially high standard of care that they claim to have.

There have been assertions that with the advent of evidence-based practice/empirically supported treatments there really is only one "best" way of treating a given condition. This is not yet the case. The vast body of

Role of
evidence-based
practice

research pointing to the importance of the personal relationship in psychotherapy suggests that it is not so simple to distinguish acceptable and negligent treatment (APA, 2006). The time may be coming, however, when the range of acceptable treatment approaches will become limited.

Some caution is necessary in applying the school-of-thought doctrine. For a school of thought to be considered acceptable, it has to be supported by a "respectable minority" in that it has a fair number of adherents. It also should have some empirical, professional, or scientific basis. There are examples of unacceptable schools of thought that lack such support. Despite the successful U.S. prosecution of Wilhelm Reich in 1947 for fraud regarding his marketing of the orgone box—a cabinet-like structure that Reich claimed could store so-called orgone energy to clients who sat in it and thus alleviate the symptoms of a number of ailments, including the common cold—there are still people practicing with the use of orgone boxes and a number of websites dedicated to advertising them (e.g., http://www.orgonomy.org, http://www.orgonomicscience.org). In a similar manner, there are websites dedicated to the sale of "immersion tanks," in which clients are suspended in warm water, for the purposes of re-creating certain prebirth experiences. An attempt at "rebirthing therapy" resulted in criminal charges against a therapist who wrapped a client tightly in blankets, ultimately resulting in the client's death (*State v. Watkins,* 2003). This case resulted in a finding of involuntary manslaughter based on "reckless indifference" and could well have been a case of malpractice litigation, with the plaintiff asserting that such treatment was a negligent deviation from accepted standards of treatment and was the proximate cause of the client's death.

A number of therapists in the 1990s became specialists in "recovered memory treatment," which dealt largely with recovered memories of childhood abuse. Although there is certainly a vast body of solid empirical literature dealing with the validity of childhood trauma and legitimate trauma-based therapy (Courtois, 1999; Pope & Brown, 1996), some of the techniques designed to "recover" the memories had scant, if any, empirical basis. Various therapists were hypnotizing clients to "break down" their defenses against repressed memories (*Ramona v. Isabella,* 1994; see also Johnston, 1997). This is an example of using unvalidated techniques that could cause a great deal of harm. In a number of these cases, for instance, plaintiffs have had some limited success in malpractice actions against therapists who "assisted" clients in "recovering" memories of sexual abuse by their family members (*Hungerford v. Jones,* 1998; *Sawyer v. Midelfort,* 1999).

There are other limitations on the school-of-thought standard of care. Practitioners in any school of thought must recognize the limitations on their own school of thought's ability to deal with certain problems and be prepared to refer clients to more appropriate services. For example, a practitioner who specializes in biofeedback would not want to use that technique with an imminently suicidal client. A physician would not want to prescribe electroconvulsive therapy for someone with Alzheimer's disease, because it is not an effective treatment for that condition; neither would a physician prescribe it for someone who has significant organic impairment, because such a treatment might cause further harm. In the same manner, a therapist would not want to embark on a course of insight-oriented depth therapy with a client who is so fragile that she or he needs some form of supportive psychotherapy. The therapist also would not want to use such depth therapy with someone who has limited intellectual functioning, because it would be ineffective. Note that for any form of nontraditional treatment informed consent becomes especially important (Frank, Gupta, & McGlynn, 2008).

Finally, an entire school of thought can be negligent because its approach is unnecessarily risky (e.g., treating a suicidal client with a highly confrontational approach) (*Helling v. Carey,* 1974). In addition, of course, professionals must be proficient in whatever approach or school of thought they are using as a basis for their work; they must know what they are doing and apply the approach correctly.

We have noted that the standard of care is doing what a reasonably careful practitioner would do under the circumstances but have not considered what the phrase "under the circumstances" means in malpractice. In an emergency, for example, there may be no opportunity to conduct the same range of tests that would ordinarily be possible. This does not excuse the failure to prepare for emergencies. Psychologists must have the appropriate materials, equipment, or support for unexpected events and refer clients to other professionals when that is appropriate (Packman, Andalibian, Eudy, Howard, & Bongar, 2009).

The "under the circumstances" concept may also apply when special facts make strict adherence to ordinary standards unnecessarily confining. For example, as a general rule, a therapist needs to maintain firm boundaries and make clear to a client that their relationship is one of therapy, not one of friends or teammates. Consider, however, a therapist who has a resistant adolescent client who happens to be an excellent basketball player. Shooting a few hoops with that client may be perfectly appropriate as long as the therapist notes what the expected boundaries might be and why he or she is departing from the standard practice (O'Laughlin, 2001). Practitioners need to document why they acted in a nontypical manner, with, for example, a statement in the client's chart describing why they took the action they did. In our example, the practitioner should note that the client was resistant and that the basketball playing was a way of overcoming the resistance.

In the past, a *locality rule*—stating that the standard of care was defined by the quality of practice in the psychologist's specific geographic location— was commonly applied in malpractice suits (Sorrel, 2010). In theory, at least, the practice of therapy in a large metropolitan area with many available resources may not be applicable to therapy in a rural area that has few available resources. The locality rule is still followed in some form in a minority of jurisdictions, but the concept has been largely discredited (Lewis, Gohagan, & Merenstein, 2007). Courts generally apply a national standard in which practitioners are expected to be aware of appropriate practice, whether in a large metropolitan area or a small village.

Proving the Standard of Care

The question of determining what a reasonably prudent practitioner would do under the circumstances is a critical element in any malpractice case. In a few cases, it is apparent: A therapist who has sex with a client clearly has acted beyond what is professionally acceptable. In most cases, the courts rely on expert witnesses to describe what is professionally acceptable practice

(Ash, 2010). Formal professional standards and publications may also be helpful in defining the standard of care (Recupero, 2008).

The use of expert witnesses is intended to help the jury understand professional and scientific issues that are beyond the understanding of the lay public. Sometimes, however, it leads to a "battle of experts" in which one mental health professional testifies that what the defendant did is perfectly acceptable, whereas another says that it is outside any professionally accepted practice.

The problem of having experts testify in regard to the standard of care is illustrated by a case in which a defendant was referred for a pretrial examination of competency following a charge of aggravated assault. Although he was found competent to stand trial and criminally responsible, the psychologists and psychiatrists believed that he had borderline personality disorder and recommended that he receive treatment in the future. He was discharged from the hospital after approximately one month, pleaded guilty, and was placed on probation with mandatory therapy as a condition. Approximately 14 months after his discharge, he killed several family members and himself. A surviving sister filed suit against the hospital, alleging negligent diagnosis. A psychiatrist testified as an expert witness that the hospital was negligent because it failed to accurately diagnose the fact that this young man suffered from a "negative Oedipus complex," and maintained that had this situation accurately been diagnosed the tragedy would have been averted. This testimony was unpersuasive because of a reasonably clear standard of care for conducting such assessments and well-documented evidence that the staff adhered to these standards.

It is important that the triers of fact (judges and juries) not be misled into believing that there is only one way in which a particular treatment can be carried out or in which a particular battery of psychological assessments can be conducted. Practitioners and the legal system appropriately take into account individual differences in approach, administration, and interpretation. All clients are not the same, and all clinicians are not the same. The treatment plan must take into account individual differences.

Any insistence on a rigid, cut-and-dried approach to psychological assessment and intervention does not accurately reflect the current state of psychological practice. It is critical that triers of fact understand this principle. Expert witnesses play an important role in helping juries and judges see the range of legitimate care in psychology.

The professional literature may also help establish a standard of care. Not everything written is authoritative, of course, but literature accepted by the defendant (or, in a few cases, even written by the defendant) or demonstrated as authoritative may also be used to establish good practice or the standard of care (Recupero, 2008).

Another form of evidence about the standard of care are the standards officially adopted by professional organizations. For example, the standards and guidelines promulgated by such professional organizations as APA (2006) may sometimes be viewed as formal establishment of such standards. There is a good argument that the mental health profession should promulgate documents that can address standards of care in various disciplines of psychology (Hedges, 2007). These standards certainly can be flexible enough to account for individual variations in practice style while at the same time stress the essentials of the practice in an area.

Some individuals maintain that the more standards and guidelines there are, the more ammunition a clever plaintiff's attorney has to use against therapists (Recupero, 2008). In the absence of such standards, though, juries will be left without sensible professional guidance when they have to apply the standard of care in malpractice cases. It is a mistake to believe that because only the formal standards of the APA Ethics Code are enforceable, and the principles, or guidelines, are aspirational, they do not have to follow the guidelines. If there is litigation, the therapist is sure to be asked why she or he did not follow the guidelines, and, absent extraordinary circumstances, the answer often appears to a trier of fact (judge or jury) to be defensive and unpersuasive.

Expert witnesses often have some documented body of literature, commonly based on research, clinical practice, guidelines, standards, or codes of ethics, that provides the basis for their testimony regarding standard of care. Avoid the idiosyncratic standard-of-care pronouncements of so-called experts described earlier in the example dealing with the negative Oedipus complex. An attorney representing a defendant psychologist in such a case should demand that the plaintiff's expert specify the body of literature on which that expert is opining that the defendant psychologist deviated from the standard of care.

Hindsight bias also works against the professional in malpractice cases (Wexler & Schopp, 1989). After something has occurred, it is always easier to go back and point out what people have "obviously missed" or that there must be a causal connection (not just a correlation) between a mistake and a bad outcome. Once an unfortunate act has occurred (e.g., a client commits suicide, or assaults someone), it is very easy for an expert witness to review the record and find something that was missed or not done properly. It should be clear that the standard of care is based on what the practitioner knew *at the time*, not what someone looking back on the situation with the benefit of hindsight states that it should have been.

CAUSATION

Negligence, regardless of how far it deviates from good practice, results in liability only if the plaintiff can demonstrate that the negligence *caused* a legally recognizable injury. Causation is frequently a major issue in mental health malpractice cases because the cause of a mental injury is often hard to pin down. The plaintiff has the burden of proof. If it is not possible to determine, directly or by implication, what caused the injury, the plaintiff loses.

In establishing causation, experts again play an important role. Experts are commonly called to testify whether, in their professional judgment, an injury or harm was a result of (i.e., caused by) the therapist's negligent treatment. These are frequently professional judgments about which there are reasonable disagreements, resulting in the judge or jury having to decide the complicated question of causation.

Lawyers commonly divide causation into two parts: (a) *causation in fact* (also called *but-for causation*) and (b) *proximate* or *legal causation. Causation in fact* means that the injury would not have occurred "but for" the negligence of the defendant—for example, the pedestrian would not have been hit but for the defendant's negligence in running the red light. *Proximate* or *legal causation* is an elusive and difficult concept that in essence means that there was a sufficient nexus or legal connection between the defendant's negligence and the plaintiff's injury. Not to simplify the concept too much, it is a way of saying that there has to be some reasonably close or direct connection between the negligence and the injury (*Williamson v. Liptzin,* 2000).

The difficulty of proving causation and the attendant difficulty of a judge or jury making a determination of causation are demonstrated by the case of a psychologist who was seeing a woman in therapy who complained of depression, loss of appetite, nausea, and headaches. The therapist told her it was not necessary to have a physical exam, that the physical symptoms were all related to the depression. In 3 months, the woman needed to be hospitalized and was diagnosed with Hodgkin's disease. She died 1 month later. The family sued the psychologist, maintaining that the standard of care dictated that he refer her for a full medical workup given her symptoms and that his failure to do so was the proximate cause of her death. A psychologist retained by the plaintiff testified that this failure to refer was a deviation from the accepted standard of care. The physician retained by the defense stated that early intervention would not have been effective in saving the woman's life because she suffered from a particularly virulent form of Hodgkin's disease that would not have responded even to the most aggressive treatment. The physician retained by the plaintiff contended that early intervention could have saved her life. The judge found that the psychologist was negligent in failing to refer the woman for a physical examination but that the plaintiff had not carried the burden of demonstrating that the failure to refer was the proximate cause of her death. *Causation* requires that the negligence has to be a major contributing factor to the illness or injury.

It is important for practitioners to rule out any physical condition that could either be causing or related to certain mental health problems. The same holds for the physiological effect of certain substances. As an example, panic attacks or other forms of severe anxiety can be related to a thyroid disorder or to some kind of hormonal imbalance. Depression, as well, can be related to thyroid problems. Even if a practitioner is not intimately familiar with the psychological presentation of many different mental disorders, she or he needs to be familiar enough at least to know when to refer a client for a medical consultation prior to undertaking therapy.

There are many pitfalls when a plaintiff is trying to assert that the practitioner's behavior is the cause of harm or injury. The causes of emotional and psychological injuries are especially difficult to pinpoint. Clients come to therapy with various mental and emotional problems at the outset, which raises the issue of causation in that there is a preexisting injury or a particular sensitivity or susceptibility to additional injury.

DAMAGES

The monetary damages in mental health malpractice cases vary considerably depending on the nature of the malpractice claim. Both economic and noneconomic compensatory damages, however, are common in malpractice cases. In many mental health malpractice cases there is no physical injury, but significant damages are still possible. Consider a hypothetical case in which there has been a wrongful breach of confidentiality whereby a therapist has revealed private information to a client's employer, resulting in the client's dismissal from her job. The damages may comprise not only the lost earnings from the job but would also include the potential for substantial emotional suffering, embarrassment, possibly a loss of reputation, and perhaps the cost of additional therapy.

When there is physical injury, damages may be considerably greater. Consider a personal injury case in which a therapist has ignored a believable suicidal threat and negligently failed to provide appropriate treatment, resulting in the suicide of the client. In such a case, damages will likely be awarded for medical expenses, the loss of earning capacity of the client, pain and suffering, and emotional distress. The spouse of an injured or deceased client may sometimes be awarded damages for loss of services (companionship, sexual relations, and affection).

Some of these compensatory damages in malpractice cases can be determined with specificity. Past medical expenses or lost wages to date may be fairly clear. Other expenses are somewhat speculative; for example, future medical expenses or the value of wages likely to be lost in the future are predictions of the future course of the plaintiff's care and recovery. Other damages, most notably noneconomic damages for pain and suffering, are highly speculative. Juries (or judges, when the case is tried without a jury) have considerable latitude in determining the appropriate value of the pain and suffering. Such discretion is not unlimited, however, and judges or appellate courts are empowered to reduce or reverse excessive damages. Noneconomic damages tend to fall within ranges that experienced insurance adjustors and trial lawyers can predict with some degree of accuracy.

Punitive damages are generally permitted in malpractice when there has been outrageous conduct, but they are not common. Such damages may be warranted, for example, when a therapist's repeated sexual involvement with a client during therapy resulted in the client's deterioration and hospitalization.

Nominal damages are usually not sufficient to support recovery by the injured plaintiff in negligence cases, although they may be sufficient to "win" in intentional torts. (Nominal damages are a small amount—say, $1—to show that the plaintiff was right but that there was not an actual loss.)

DEFENSES

Many defenses are available to the practitioner in a malpractice case. Some *procedural defenses,* for example, preclude a court from hearing a claim. In others, called *substantive defenses,* the practitioner argues that one of the required elements of a tort action, such as causation, is missing. There also are a number of legal immunities. For example, an expert witness may have immunity for testimony given in court, even if it is otherwise defamatory (Greenberg, Shuman, Feldman, Middleton, & Ewing, 2007).

Complete defenses defeat the tort liability that the plaintiff is seeking so that there is no liability. There also are *partial defenses,* which do not preclude damages but reduce damages for which the therapist is responsible. The notable example is *comparative negligence* (the plaintiff's own negligence contributed to the injury discussed in more detail later in this chapter), which can be important in mental health liability cases.

The nature of the defenses available, of course, depends on the cause of action on which liability is claimed. For example, in a hypothetical federal civil rights case (i.e., based on Title 42, U.S. Code § 1983, "Civil Action for Deprivation of Rights") by a state prisoner claiming a constitutional violation because of failure to provide sound psychotherapy, the prison and the therapist could defend by claiming that there was not "deliberate indifference" to the prisoner's condition (the federal constitutional standard for liability; Parry, 2010). Such a defense would not be available in an ordinary negligence malpractice case.

A case based on contract requires that there be an agreement (offer and acceptance) creating legal duties. Therefore, a defense might be that there was no offer; this would not be relevant to tort cases where liability is not based on the existence of a contract.

In a battery case, for example, a defense that there was not "intent" to strike the defendant would be available, but because intent is not required for a negligence action it would not be a viable defense for negligence. Because negligence is the common basis for mental health malpractice, the discussion that follows focuses on defenses for negligence.

In any cause of action the plaintiff is responsible for proving, by a preponderance of the evidence (more likely than not), each of the elements of that legal action. In a negligence case, for example, that would mean proving duty, breach of duty, causation, and injury. If the plaintiff fails to prove *any* one of the elements, the entire case fails and the defendant wins. In negligence, for example, failure to demonstrate that the practitioner caused the injury would defeat the claim for liability, even though the practitioner had in fact clearly been negligent. In the case noted earlier in this chapter of the woman with Hodgkin's disease, for instance, although the psychologist was found negligent (he failed to refer her for a timely physical evaluation), this was not seen as the proximate cause of her death.

Although the plaintiff generally has the burden of proving all of the elements of a claim by a preponderance of the evidence, in the event of affirmative defenses (e.g., self-defense) and some immunity claims (e.g. governmental or sovereign immunity), the burden of proof may be on the defense to prove that the exception to liability is warranted. Similarly, when the defendant/practitioner is trying to establish that the negligence of the plaintiff/client contributed to the injury, the defense may be required to prove both the plaintiff's negligence and how it contributed to the injury.

In the next section, we summarize the defenses commonly used in malpractice cases.

Procedural Defenses

Examples of procedural defenses include the following:

- The court does not have legal jurisdiction over this case or over the defendant. A court cannot hear a case unless it has both *subject matter jurisdiction* (i.e., it is permitted by law to hear this kind of case) and *personal jurisdiction* (i.e., the court has sufficient contact with the defendant to justify exercising jurisdiction over the defendant). A Pennsylvania state court cannot, for example, claim jurisdiction over a psychologist from California for, say, treating a client in Massachusetts when the psychologist has not had any contact with Pennsylvania.
- The *statute of limitations* (the time following an injury during which a defendant may file an action) has expired, and the court may no longer entertain the claim. States place limits on the time during which malpractice claims can be brought (Parry, 2010). They also define circumstances (e.g., the plaintiff being a minor or incompetent) under which the statute of limitation is *tolled*, or stops running temporarily.
- The specific claim that the plaintiff is making is not legally recognized. Not every wrong has a remedy. The law recognizes only specific causes of action, and a case will ordinarily be dismissed if the plaintiff's claim does not fall within one of these actions.

Substantive Defenses

Many of the substantive defenses fall into the category of "one required element of negligence liability does not exist." Indeed, in most malpractice lawsuits this is what the case is about.

- *There was no duty to this person (the plaintiff).* There has to have been a professional relationship between the plaintiff and the defendant. Often the relationship is clear because there is a mutual expectation that such a relationship exists. However, when that expectation is not clear, the defense of "no duty to this person" will be significant. There is some trend to expand the persons to whom a therapist owes a duty to include identifiable third parties against whom a client has made believable threats (*Tarasoff v. Regents of the University of California,* 1976, a case we discuss in detail in Chapter 6). This extended-duty concept, however, remains limited. For the most part, negligence liability is limited to the client with whom the defendant has a professional relationship.

- *The duty of reasonable care under the circumstances was not breached (the professional acted as a reasonably prudent practitioner).* The very essence of negligence liability is a practitioner's obligation to act as a reasonably prudent professional would under the circumstances. There are non-negligent errors that should not give rise to liability, so the plaintiff must prove that the mistake was outside reasonable professional judgment.

  The question of whether there has been adherence to the standard of care is one for the trier of fact (the jury or judge) to decide. Thus, a lay body is ultimately making a judgment on the adequacy of professional practice. The plaintiff has the burden of proving, usually with expert witnesses, that the practice of the professional was not consistent with the standard of care. The defense may challenge the plaintiff's expert testimony, so the defense also almost always calls one or more experts to counter the plaintiff's experts.

- *There was no injury.* Proving that there was some injury is ordinarily not difficult. Proving its severity and knowing how the injury should be valued are difficult in mental health malpractice. The plaintiff must prove the harm and provide evidence of its severity.

  For pain and suffering and other noneconomic damages, plaintiffs present evidence (including their own testimony) of the nature of the injury and how it affected their lives. Expert witnesses may be helpful in providing some information about the nature of certain injuries or conditions. Ultimately, however, the jury is left with the task of trying to put a monetary value on noneconomic elements of the injury.

- *The negligence did not cause the injury.* Causation is a difficult element for the plaintiff to prove in many mental health malpractice cases. These cases often involve people who, independent of the malpractice, are distressed and who have distorted perceptions, difficult interpersonal relations, and impairments in their ability to appraise reality. The plaintiff often has to demonstrate that the impairments did not exist independent of the negligence and were not due to the natural progression of the plaintiff's mental health condition itself. The plaintiff may seek to demonstrate that the clinician's negligence exacerbated the preexisting condition, but it may be difficult to demonstrate that the worsening of the condition was caused by the negligence and not by some other factor.

The proof of causation does not have to be by direct evidence but can be by implication. A review of the client's history, for example, may suggest that the client was doing better and had a severe setback only following an error by the therapist. Good documentation by the therapist may be helpful in answering the causation, often in the therapist's favor. The difficulty in proving causation is one of the reasons that mental health malpractice cases are less common than physical health cases.

In practice, there may not always be this nice separation of elements (duty, breach, causation, and injury) in the minds of jurors, especially when the damages are great. Poythress (1990) studied this phenomenon and concluded that there is a tendency to confuse standard-of-care issues with other elements of negligence based on the severity of damages. He suggested in some cases having bifurcated trials for liability and damages.

Other Defenses

In negligence, the most common affirmative defenses are *contributory/comparative negligence* (which we discuss in the next section) and *assumption of the risk* (the plaintiff voluntarily and knowingly agreed to take the risk of injury). Other specific defenses are mentioned in this section.

In intentional torts, the primary additional defenses are *consent, self-defense,* and *necessity.* The informed-consent process is a mechanism to ensure that the defense of consent is available for battery and other intentional torts (Slovenko, 1998). Self-defense is available when the defendant (psychologist) reasonably believes he or she is in danger. It is defined as the amount of force reasonable to defend oneself under the circumstances. Necessity is involved when it is essential to invade the legal interests of someone in an emergency to avoid great harm to persons or property; for example, knocking a bystander out of the way to prevent a gunman from firing into a crowd would be an excusable necessity. Similarly, holding an immediately dangerous client to keep him from detonating a bomb could be a necessity defense.

The doctrine of *sovereign immunity* may protect state institutions and their employees from some liability, or require that the injured person go through an administrative process instead of the tort system. A client who is injured in a state mental hospital, for example, may be required to present the claim for damages to a special department or court of claims rather than to an ordinary court. These processes vary from state to state. The Federal Tort Claims Act (2010) provides a specific mechanism for those injured by federal institutions and employees. In this act, there is a limited waiver of the federal government's sovereign immunity when employees are negligent within the scope of their employment. Most states also waive sovereign immunity to varying degrees.

In addition, there are a number of immunities that protect clinicians from liability even if significant mistakes were made. This immunity is often related to performing certain functions (Huffman, 2008). For example, testimony in court, participating in the civil commitment process, and reporting child abuse all have immunities in most states (Hall & Resnick, 2008). This immunity, however, usually does not extend where there is bad faith by the therapist.

COMPARATIVE NEGLIGENCE

The defense of comparative negligence arises when the plaintiff was partly responsible for the accident or harm. In most states this is a partial defense that reduces damages instead of eliminating liability altogether.

The law recognizes the basic unfairness of requiring clinicians to pay the damages when clients have contributed to their own injuries. Most states, therefore, ask the trier of fact (a judge or jury) to apportion how much of the negligence is due to the therapist's actions or inactions and how much is due to the client. The amount that the client contributed is then subtracted from the portion due to the therapist's behavior, resulting in the final judgment. When the client has suffered $100,000 of damages, and the jury decides that the therapist is liable for 60% of the damages and the client (due to his or her noncompliance with directions) for 40% of the damages, the amount of the final judgment against the therapist is $60,000; that is, the $100,000 is reduced by the amount that the plaintiff contributed to the injury (40%). This process, of course, again asks the jury to undertake a difficult assessment of relative responsibility, one that can be done only roughly.

This is called *comparative negligence* because it compares the relative fault of the plaintiff and the defendant (Behnke, 2000). It replaced the older *contributory negligence* in which if the trier of fact determined that the client in any material way contributed to the injury, the case was essentially dismissed (Slovenko, 2005).

Should the therapist be responsible when a client refuses to adhere to the established treatment plan? For example, suppose a therapist has referred a client for a medication evaluation and the client does not go and subsequently is harmed because he has not taken the medication.

A therapist must be careful to always document not only treatment progress but also any times and ways in which a client is noncompliant. For example, if a client did not do regular "homework" in a cognitive behavioral course of therapy, that should be documented. Another example is when a client does not follow through on referrals. If a client is on medication but deviates from the prescribed dosing regimen, that may contribute to any injury sustained. These facts, if well documented, can assist the therapist if the client sues for malpractice. They can help demonstrate that the harm, in part, came from the client's noncompliance with treatment.

PRACTICAL SUGGESTIONS

1. Quality, ethical, and careful professional practice, consistent with accepted standards, is the most important element in avoiding malpractice. Psychologists need only to have acted within the range of what a reasonable practitioner would have done under the circumstances. Bad results, even mistakes, do not prove negligence.

2. Practice only within your existing competencies, and be up to date in any area of practice you undertake. Be familiar with the current literature and ethical standards that would affect your practice.

3. Therapists may choose from any number of legitimate schools of thought so long as a respectable number of therapists adhere to this school and it is supported by legitimate empirical, professional, or scientific bases.

4. Hold yourself out as a specialist only if you have advanced and specialized training. The law will hold you to a higher level of expertise if you claim to have it.

5. Expert witnesses are usually called to help the jury understand professional and scientific issues in determining what is professionally acceptable practice and whether injuries were caused by the negligence of a psychologist. It is very helpful if the psychologist has clearly documented diagnosis and treatment decisions in the client's record.

6. Professional standards and guidelines promulgated by such professional organizations as APA may not define completely what is beyond acceptable practice, but they often contribute to such a definition, and psychologists should be aware of all such guidelines that affect their practices.

7. It may be reassuring to mental health professionals to remember that there are many defenses available to the practitioner in a malpractice case. Procedural defenses preclude a court from hearing a claim, substantive defenses are usually based on the claim that an element of a tort action is missing, and immunities may excuse what would otherwise be a tort.

3

The Professional Relationship and Consent

At the core of most malpractice cases is the professional relationship between psychologist and client. In this chapter, we consider how that relationship begins and ends and the critical place of informed consent in the resulting legal duties. In subsequent chapters, we consider the limited circumstances in which therapists owe legal duties to those who are not their clients.

It is the professional therapist–client relationship that imposes the legal duties in a malpractice case. A friendship or idle conversation between a therapist and another person generally does not create a professional relationship. The following hypothetical case is an example of a nonrelationship. A family therapy expert was consulted by a psychologist about some possible abuse issues in the family the psychologist was seeing. The expert told the psychologist that the behaviors described were consistent with those she had seen in several other cases involving abuse. The expert had never seen the client, and did not make reference to the client, but only commented on the consistency of certain behaviors. The client filed suit after discovering that the psychologist had consulted the expert. The case against the "expert" was dismissed because there was no professional relationship between the client and the expert. This example case emphasizes that the nature of professional relationships should be clarified and documented.

PROFESSIONAL RELATIONSHIP

If a practitioner and client meet and decide that they will continue in a process of treatment or assessment, then clearly a professional relationship has been established. If a psychologist talks to someone on the phone or a hotline, is that a professional relationship? There are times when someone other than the client is seen for a collateral session—a therapist might see the wife of a client, for example, on a few occasions to assist the husband's therapy. In this instance, does the wife now have a professional relationship with the therapist (Belar & Deardorff, 2009)?

A professional relationship is generally established when a reasonable person would assume from all of the circumstances and the conduct of the therapist that a professional relationship exists. That is, there is a mutually shared expectation that the initial contact, e.g., by telephone, will lead to further professional contact (*Oregon v. Miller*, 1985).

This is not a precise standard for practitioners to apply. For that reason, therapists should be very clear with anyone they are seeing exactly what the nature of the relationship is. It is often helpful to discuss how long it is anticipated the relationship will last. Clarity of relationships is particularly important when the therapist does not intend for there to be a professional relationship. The therapist should specify, preferably in writing, for example, whether the expected services are consultation, a diagnostic assessment for the purpose of further treatment, diagnostic assessment with a report going to a third party, time-limited treatment (as sometimes dictated by managed care companies), or longer term therapy.

Even without a specific statement that a professional relationship exists, there may be an implicit relationship that arises from the conduct of the therapist. The therapist needs to be sensitive to the fact that certain individuals may perceive a treatment relationship even if one does not exist. This was illustrated by *Thayer v. OrRico* (2003), in which the plaintiff (an employee at a mental health clinic) consulted a therapist at the clinic without making actual appointments and without being billed for the visits. A claim of malpractice ensued, and the psychologist's defense was that no professional relationship existed with the employee. The court said there might have been such a relationship. Some of the issues were whether the plaintiff had consulted the therapist for treatment, whether the therapist's recommendations could be regarded as part of a treatment plan, and whether the therapist did anything that suggested to the client the establishment of a therapist–client relationship. The therapist did give advice to the plaintiff and in fact even suggested that she stop her current medication and take herbal supplements. The court considered the plaintiff's claim that "a genuine issue of material fact existed" (for the jury to decide) regarding whether there was a professional relationship.

Special complications may occur when the therapy relationship arises because of emergency treatment. Both the common law and statutes, including the federal Emergency Medical Treatment and Active Labor Act of 1986 (EMTALA, 1986), impose duties on emergency services personnel to examine and stabilize clients. EMTALA is also intended to prevent the receiving hospital from dumping the client on another hospital for economic reasons. Although EMTALA requires only that the client be "stabilized," in some circumstances it is possible that a therapy relationship arising from the emergency would require that the therapist provide for some kind of follow-up care.

In *Davis v. Lhim* (1983), an unusual case, a client was admitted to the emergency room of a psychiatric hospital in a very agitated, drug-induced state. While in the emergency room, he was mumbling about wanting to kill his mother because she would not give him money to buy drugs. This was documented in the emergency room notes. The client's mother visited with him on several occasions while he was in the hospital, and he never made any threats to her. After a brief stay, he was recommended for convalescent leave. There was apparently no effective plan for follow-up care. Approximately 18 months later, the client began hallucinating again, was fending off the voices with a shotgun, and when his mother tried to take the gun away from him, he accidentally shot and killed her. The mother's estate sued the hospital for negligence, asserting, among other things, that hospital staff should have warned the mother of the risk of violence. The jury determined that a therapy relationship existed, and the events between the time of the client's release and the murder were foreseeable, so the jury found that the psychiatrist's negligence was the proximate cause of the mother's death. (Ultimately, the case was reversed on appeal based on sovereign immunity; *Canon v. Thumudo*, 1988.)

ENDING THE THERAPY RELATIONSHIP AND ABANDONMENT

Just as it is important to know when a therapy relationship begins, it is equally important to know when it ends. Clinicians cannot simply announce that the relationship has ended. Ethical and legal standards require that the psychologist see to a continuity of care for the client. Failure to do so may constitute *abandonment*. There are ethical and legal ways of terminating a therapy relationship; termination must be undertaken carefully and thoughtfully (Vasquez, Bingham, & Barnett, 2008).

Although there are cases in which clinicians have completely and literally abandoned clients (Parry, 2010; Smith, 1986), there are many more in which a lack of continuity of care created misunderstanding, neglect, or poor follow-through whereby clients were harmed. These are technically forms of negligence but are commonly called abandonment. In *Marshall v. Klebanov* (2006), Mrs. Marshall committed suicide 2 days before a scheduled appointment with her psychiatrist. At her intake session, she had told the psychiatrist, Dr. Klebanov, about previous suicide attempts, as well as her current suicidal ideation and her treatment for depression. He diagnosed her with major depressive disorder and scheduled another appointment. What happened at the next appointment is in dispute. Apparently Klebanov believed that Marshall needed to be seen weekly but did not schedule the next session after the disputed one for another month. Mrs. Marshall did in fact commit suicide. The plaintiff's claim was that this month-long delay was, in fact, abandonment. The court was concerned that such a long period of time had elapsed between the two sessions that the doctor was not in a position to evaluate whether or not the client may have been deteriorating and becoming more overtly suicidal. The court held that this could have been abandonment and that it was for the jury to decide whether it was negligence.

There should be a clear, mutual understanding between therapist and client included in the informed consent about what will be done in the case of limitations of services (e.g., by managed care). The clinician needs to inform the client, for example, of the number of sessions authorized by the client's insurance company, the treatment plan that will be used within that number, the clinician's willingness to appeal if the clinical needs of the client exceed the limited number of sessions, and what will happen if the appeal is turned down. Clients should be informed that, if necessary, the therapist will attempt to refer them to a reduced-fee or free clinic and will continue seeing her or him until an effective transfer can be made.

One frequent problem is a client who does not pay the fee. Therapists cannot simply drop a client for failure to pay. No one expects the therapist to provide free services indefinitely, but the termination of treatment needs to be done in a way that is sensitive and will not harm the client. It is helpful to have a carefully designed plan put into place ahead of time that addresses this.

On a related note, collection of fees must be undertaken with care. The American Psychological Association's (APA's; 2010) "Ethical Principles of Psychologists and Code of Conduct" (http://www.apa.org/ethics/code/index.aspx) directs psychologists to attempt to work out a repayment schedule for clients who are in arrears before turning the matter over to a collection agency.

Another circumstance in which a claim of abandonment might arise is when therapists feel they can no longer work effectively with a client. This may be due to a lack of progress or merely some personal difficulties between the therapist and the client. In such cases, there is an ethical as well as a legal duty to refer—the therapist cannot, of course, just dump the client. There must be clear documentation of a referral and a good faith effort to see that the referral is followed up. This does not mean that the therapist has to track down the client and make sure that the client has contacted the new therapist; however, it does necessitate something more than a therapist telling a client that he is retiring and that the client should follow up on treatment, without providing any referral information to the client (Vasquez et al., 2008).

When managed care limits the number of times that a therapist can see a client, it creates a dilemma for the therapist. On the one hand, the therapist might see the need for further treatment. On the other hand, she or he cannot afford to see managed care clients pro bono. Some of this can be handled with a carefully crafted informed consent discussing the allowed number of sessions and making advance arrangements with the client about what will happen should further treatment be necessary. Such arrangements may help avoid ethical and legal problems, but they must be handled with careful consideration of the client's individual situation (Appelbaum, 1996).

If a psychologist's clinical judgment dictates that the client needs further treatment, it often behooves the therapist both ethically and legally to file an appeal with the client's insurance company. There is at least some authority to suggest that health care providers may be responsible for appealing the denial of benefits that they believe are necessary (*Wickline v. State of California*, 1986). Of course, if an appeal is denied, the therapist still needs to take the responsibility for referring the client to another provider, such as a community mental health center or a free clinic.

A therapist can terminate a client's therapy for failure to adhere to the treatment plan, such as not following up on a referral for a medication consult or frequently missing or canceling sessions. It is important, however, that the client be informed of a therapist's concerns and given an opportunity to discuss the issues. As always, when therapy is terminated the practitioner must take reasonable steps to have the client transferred or referred to another therapist, as the client's condition warrants. Hedges (2007) suggested that the therapist should attempt to obtain the client's signature verifying that he or she has discussed the issues with the therapist and knows why he or she is being referred to someone else. Again, documentation is critical here, as is consultation with a trusted and competent colleague and an attorney.

The client must also be given time to thoroughly process the termination. As part of the documentation, the chart should include a full discussion of the termination, for example, what aspects of the treatment plan the client did not follow, the kinds of therapeutic services needed by the client, and where the client may locate such resources. Special circumstances, including psychotherapy with children, require additional caution in terminating therapy and in communicating with not only the client but also others (e.g., parents) interested in the therapy relationship (Rappleyea, Harris, White, & Simon, 2009).

INFORMED CONSENT

Informed consent is not only an important legal concept but also a central ethical practice (Section 3.10, APA [2010] Ethics Code). In addition, it can be a significant element in therapist–client communication. Informed-consent rules implement and protect some of the most important values of psychotherapy: privacy and client protection. Practitioners should, therefore, pay attention to these legal rules and structure their work to implement best practices (Hedges, 2007).

Too often mental health practitioners ignore the doctrine of informed consent (Berg, Appelbaum, Parker, & Lidz, 2001). Therapists may believe that clients have limited competency to understand such documents or feel paternalistic and believe that the clients cannot make decisions that are in their own best interests. Some use such a consent form mechanically, feeling that having a client sign it automatically protects them from liability. These mistakes carry legal and ethical risks.

The informed-consent process should be undertaken early in the therapy relationship, and it can often be a significant part of creating that relationship. Therapists ordinarily need to obtain informed consent and document it early enough so that the client is aware of the parameters and limits of the treatment before too much time has passed. Therapists should be sure that the client is competent to understand the issues and have this documented in the chart. The first session is a good time to discuss the informed-consent document. Sending it home with the client to review and bring to the next session for discussion is also a feasible technique. The document is something to be discussed in therapy, not just a paper to be filed in the chart.

Failure to Obtain Informed Consent

Informed-consent issues are not uncommon in mental health malpractice claims. Although a number of cases involve failure to obtain informed consent for somatic treatments such as electroconvulsive therapy and medication, and some of the behavioral therapies involving aversive stimuli or implosive methods, the same principles of consent apply to psychotherapy and to psychological assessment. A number of complaints to licensing boards and ethics committees, and malpractice claims, could be avoided if all practitioners took precautions to obtain a thorough informed consent to whatever the assessment or intervention might be. If a client has been given sufficient knowledge, voluntarily consents to an intervention, and is competent to make that decision, then the risk of liability related to informed consent is small.

Failure to obtain informed consent ordinarily manifests itself in negligence related to the sufficiency of information given the client. Infrequently, the failure to obtain informed consent may result in breach-of-contract or battery suits. The assertions in breach-of-contract suits could contend that the therapist promised certain results and they did not occur. Although most therapists would never promise a particular result, offering certain pop forms of psychotherapy that promise immediate results for a wide variety of conditions (all the way from phobias to grief reactions) would place therapists at some risk for breach of contract. For instance, one such treatment listed more than 20 conditions in a brochure and proclaimed on the cover "There Is a Cure!" It then described the treatment protocol, which consisted of tapping certain points on the body while humming a tune.

Competency to Consent

The informed-consent process assumes that a client has legal capacity to consent to treatment. Two things may interfere with the legitimacy of that assumption: (a) mental incompetence and (b) age.

Mental health professionals should assess the client's mental competence to consent to treatment. The nature of the population seeking psychotherapy means that varying degrees of mental or emotional problems may interfere with the client's competence. In *Zinermon v. Burch* (1990), the U.S. Supreme Court held that consent given by an incompetent client is not legally binding and may not provide the legal basis for holding the client in an institution. Clients who are formally adjudicated incompetent will have guardians making decisions for them, but more frequently the degree of impairment in an individual client seen by the clinician may not be so severe as to have resulted in the appointment of a guardian. The practitioner should tailor the consent to the needs of the specific situation; this is particularly true when a client may have some form of cognitive impairment. In that case, the psychologist should determine that a client is minimally competent to consent to treatment and, if competent, that the information is provided in a way that takes the impairment into account.

It is a well-established axiom that one competency does not fit all (*Indiana v. Edwards,* 2008). Competency to stand trial, for instance, may not necessarily mean that that same client is competent to make a treatment decision. Put broadly, to be competent to consent to treatment, the client will have to understand what giving consent means, be able to process in some reasonable way the information that is provided, and come to a conclusion that is communicated to the practitioner. Severe delusions and the like may make it impossible to consent to treatment. An instrument that is very helpful in assessing competency to consent to treatment is the MacArthur Competence Assessment Tool for Treatment (Grisso & Appelbaum, 1998). The therapist must also assess reading level and oral vocabulary skills to be sure the client can understand the consent.

A particularly difficult dilemma regarding informed consent occurs when the clients are minor children (*Parham v. J. R.,* 1979). Issues related to treating children, including consent, are considered in Chapter 7.

The "Informed" of Informed Consent

A frequent, fundamental question is what information should be disclosed. Information to the client needs to be comprehensive enough to cover the basics but brief enough that the client will be able to understand it. Broadly stated, this is not difficult to answer: "The professional need

4 elements in
of "informed
informed consent

disclose only those risks which a reasonable person would consider material to a decision whether or not to undergo treatment" (*Jeffries v. McCague*, 1976). A lengthy document, though perhaps legally acceptable, may not serve the function if the client found it so complex that he or she could not understand it and merely signed it to get it over with.

There are differences among states' laws regarding informed consent for health care, but the similarities eclipse the differences. At the most basic level, the purpose of giving information to the client is to provide the basis for the client to make a reasonably informed judgment regarding whether to accept or reject the treatment or intervention. The common understanding is that this information should include four elements: (a) the nature of the treatment or assessment, (b) its risks and benefits, (c) alternative forms of treatment, and (d) the consequences of not receiving the treatment (*Canterbury v. Spence*, 1972).

The "fit" of these four traditional elements of informed consent to various forms of psychological intervention is not perfect. For instance, can a therapist say with any degree of certainty that treatment will be more effective if he or she performs a particular kind of psychological assessment? What risks and benefits may come about when dealing with informed consent, especially to verbal psychotherapy or psychological testing? What consequences could reasonably be anticipated from the client not agreeing to the assessment or treatment?

In *Osheroff v. Chestnut Lodge* (1985), the plaintiff had been a client at a private psychiatric hospital with a strong psychodynamic orientation and a reluctance to use medication as an adjunct to intensive psychotherapy. The client was in treatment for a period of time with no appreciable improvement. He signed himself out of the hospital and began seeing a psychiatrist, who prescribed antidepressant medication. The client felt improved within a relatively short period of time. He then sued the hospital for failure to follow a treatment that included medication. The hospital's defense was that utilization of medication was not a part of their treatment philosophy. The court nevertheless found the hospital negligent, not for failure to medicate the client but for failure to inform him that medication was an available alternative form of treatment. The client needed to know of alternative forms of treatment in order to make an informed decision.

The disclosure to clients of risks has been of particular concern. Most states have adopted an approach that requires disclosure of *material risks* (that could play a role in the decision process of a reasonable or ordinary person). In *Funk v. Feldman* (1973), for example, an anesthesiologist told a client that he might experience headaches as a result of a spinal anesthetic but failed to reveal to him that it might also cause nerve damage. This resulted in a successful suit by the client when he did in fact suffer nerve damage. In a similar way, some behaviorally oriented treatments, such as implosive therapy or aversive conditioning, may require enhanced informed consent regarding the risks and discomfort of therapy.

There are two major exceptions to the disclosure of material information to a client. The first is the *emergency exception:* When a client is in need of immediate care to prevent substantial injury and is unable to consent, temporary consent is presumed. The second exception is the *therapeutic exception,* which permits withholding information that would be harmful to the client or cause severe emotional distress. The therapeutic exception should be used rarely and carefully; it comes with a red flag warning. It does not justify not disclosing information on the basis of the concern that a client would forego the treatment. The reasons for not making disclosures must be documented, along with notations about what information was withheld. In such cases, it is often good practice to provide the family or others with the information not disclosed to the client.

Beyond the technical legal requirements for informed consent, the process is an opportunity to consider other nuts and bolts issues, such as fees (including whether a client is charged for missed sessions or sessions to which she or he arrives late); the amount of arrearage in payment that will be tolerated; and collection procedures, if any. Discussions regarding managed care restrictions on treatment should also be included when appropriate. Those discussions might include consideration of how the therapist and client will deal with the issue if a managed care organization refuses to authorize further treatment.

Practices regarding referrals and consultations, and the associated attempts to protect confidentiality, should be discussed. If the client is a minor, there needs to be a discussion about what material will be kept confidential and what material will be shared with the parent or guardian.

Hedges (2007) suggested that the issue of the client's right to terminate therapy at any time should be included as part of informed consent. He also suggested that periodic reviews be conducted of the client's progress, or lack of progress, toward certain treatment goals and that these discussions be clearly documented in the record.

More than most any other health profession, issues of confidentiality and privacy are critical to clients of psychologists (Everstine et al., 2008). The informed consent process should clearly explain to clients the limits of confidentiality in psychotherapy.

Informed Consent and Confidentiality

People generally associate absolute confidentiality with a visit to a mental health professional and seldom consider exceptions to that principle. In one recent case a police officer referred for a fitness-for-duty evaluation by his commanding officer filed an ethics complaint against the psychologist for sending a report to the referral source. The examinee contended that the psychologist had breached confidentiality by sending the report. The psychologist, of course, took the position that there was no confidentiality because the referral had come from the commanding officer, and it was apparent that a report would be sent to him. It was apparent to almost everyone except the police officer being examined, because it had not been made explicit to him.

The limits of confidentiality are elements of information that should be discussed with a client as soon as clinically feasible (Everstine et al., 2008). Some clients need to be informed that there are mandatory reporting requirements, notably including child abuse and elder abuse (Guedj, Sastre, Mullet, & Sorum, 2009). Others may need to know that there are exceptions if they put their mental state into litigation. The effect of Health Insurance Portability and Accountability Act requirements may warrant consideration of what disclosures are and are not permitted under that statute (D'Emanuele, Soshnik, & Bomash, 2009).

Group therapy and conjoint sessions raise special problems of consent regarding confidentiality and privilege. In terms of confidentiality, the presence of another party or parties makes ensuring confidentiality more difficult. Any member of group therapy might breach confidentiality, of course. There may be a group therapy contract to maintain confidentiality, but the therapist cannot assure members that other members of the group will maintain promises of confidentiality. Standard 4 of the APA (2010) Ethics Code makes it clear that the therapist should define who the client is and what the limits of confidentiality may be, and that would include the special limits of group therapy.

Privileges (the right to refuse to give courts information from the confidences of therapy) present another difficult matter (Klinka, 2009). The presence of a third party (beyond the client and therapist or therapist's assistant) traditionally has destroyed the privilege because the therapy information is no longer confidential. Other members of a therapy group may be seen as third parties, meaning that no member of the group could claim the privilege. The better view is that other group members do not destroy the therapist–client privilege. It may be necessary, however, to inform all group members, or both parties in conjoint therapy, of the relevant issues regarding privilege and confidentiality.

Conjoint therapy with spouses raises the interesting problem of the coupling of privileges. Spousal privilege exists in various forms but may prevent one spouse from being required to reveal private interspousal communications. When the communications occur with a therapist, there should be no one individual who is considered a third party, and the privilege generally should be preserved.

Therapists cannot resolve all of these problems, of course. They can take some steps to reduce the chance of major difficulties in group and conjoint therapy. They can make special efforts to explain issues of confidentiality and privilege in these therapy formats. Practitioners may also consider confidentiality and privilege in the way they maintain records.

The need for informed consent, thoughtful respect for client confidentiality, and caution in the release of information is illustrated by the following example case. Dr. N was treating a client referred to her for treatment for emotional distress after the client slipped on some ice in front of a community center. Dr. N received a subpoena for her records from the attorney representing the community center. Reasoning that the client had waived privilege by suing for emotional distress, Dr. N released the records. The client filed a complaint with the local psychology licensing board. The licensing board and court determined that Dr. N should have gotten an informed consent to possible discovery of the records at the outset of treatment or resisted the subpoena and waited for a court order to release the records.

Forensic Issues

Put simply, in most forensic work there should be little expectation of confidentiality, and that should be clear to the person being examined. This is not to say that the psychologist is free to make forensic information public—that is not the case, either. Instead, if an assessment is done for the courts that assessment will be disclosed to the court and to the involved parties. If the assessment is done for one of the parties, that information may be discoverable and subject to disclosure in court. (In some instances, the report for one side may be protected by attorney–client privilege and not subject to disclosure.)

In any event, the practitioner should clearly explain to the person being assessed what to expect in terms of confidentiality. Such disclosures are appropriate because of the common misconception that the information provided a psychologist is private. Practitioners doing forensic work should familiarize themselves with the rules of confidentiality in order to properly craft an informed consent document. For instance, it needs to be made clear to the examinee when a third party is to receive the report. In developing the proper informed consent disclosures it is appropriate for the psychologist to raise the issue with the attorney with whom the psychologist is working (Bucky, Callan, & Stricker, 2009). Clinicians need to be careful not to confuse their forensic and clinical roles, not only for purposes of informed consent but also because of concerns about harmful multiple relationships (Ebert, 2006). Standard 3.5 of the APA (2010) Ethics Code addresses issues related to multiple relationships. When a therapist has been a treating professional but is becoming a testifying expert for the client, a clear delineation of roles is essential. A psychologist should undertake this potential double role only after careful consultation with colleagues and the full consent of the client (Woody, 2002). In some circumstances, a psychologist may discover information during an examination that is important but beyond the scope of the engagement. Suppose that an examinee makes a believable suicide threat. Although the legal rules of confidentiality and obligation are somewhat unclear, the better position would seem to be that the psychologist should be free to take action, including breaching confidentiality, to prevent the suicide (Bongar, 2002) or other serious harm.

Experimental and Innovative Treatments

Therapies that use experimental techniques, or approaches that are not reasonably well established, require enhanced informed consent. Human studies conducted in most institutions, for example, are required to meet specific federal informed-consent requirements. Among other things, these include informing the subjects that they are in an experimental study and are not required to participate and may withdraw at any time without penalty. Ordinarily, an institutional review board (IRB) will vet the informed consent before permission is given for the study to commence.

The Informed Consent Process

If informed consent is seen as an opportunity to enhance communication with clients, it makes sense for the practitioner to thoughtfully develop a process of obtaining informed consent that will achieve the maximum benefit. This implies that the practitioner must review the informed consent document with the client. As we noted earlier, we believe that the document should be provided to the client in the first session, with the client given the chance to review the document at his or her leisure. Legitimate openness and a willingness to answer questions are important parts of this process. Informed consent should be regarded as an ongoing process, not as a one-time event. At the same time, as always, documentation is also critical.

PRACTICAL SUGGESTIONS

1. Know who your client is, and document what is and is not a professional relationship.
2. Never abandon clients: Make appropriate referrals if the client becomes noncompliant with therapy or refuses to pay for sessions.
3. Clinical judgment, not insurance company restrictions, should determine the length of treatment; if these conflict, file an appeal and document it. Work collaboratively with the client to design a circumscribed treatment program if limitations to treatment can be anticipated.
4. Evaluate the competency of clients to give informed consent.
5. For informed consent to take place, the client must be competent, have access to sufficient information, and make a decision freely and voluntarily. Legally and ethically, a practitioner needs to inform the client of the purpose of any assessment or intervention, the nature of the assessment or intervention, the risks and benefits of the intervention, alternative interventions that may be applicable, and the risks associated with refusal of the intervention.
6. Discussion of the limits of confidentiality is especially important in psychotherapy. The client is likely not to know what the limitations are. This can be a complex part of informed consent and should be tailored to the client's situation.
7. Discuss fully, and document carefully, disclosure issues in conjoint and group therapy.
8. There should be a clearly delineated fee arrangement spelled out in advance in the informed consent document.

4

Confidentiality and Privacy

Client privacy and confidentiality are among the most essential professional and ethical values for psychologists. Standard 4 of the American
Psychological Association's (APA's; 2010) "Ethical Principles of Psychologists and Code of Conduct" (http://www.apa.org/ethics/code/index.aspx)
addresses issues regarding confidentiality. In this chapter, we consider the
legal issues raised by these concepts. We consider the related matter of testimonial privileges in Chapter 8.

PRIVACY, CONFIDENTIALITY, AND PRIVILEGE

It is helpful to clarify terms. *Privacy* is a generic concept that certain information belongs to the individual and should not be disclosed. *Confidentiality* refers to the ethical and legal obligation of a professional to maintain the
private communications concerning a client, absent a specific justification
for releasing the information. *Privilege*—or, more accurately, *testimonial
privilege*—is the special legal right to keep from courts (or other bodies) confidential communications from certain relationships, including therapist–

client communications. It may, for example, prevent a therapist from being called as a witness in court to repeat what a client said in therapy.

Confidentiality is not absolute; there are many exceptions to confidentiality rights. Efforts to claim absolute protection of therapy communications have failed. For example, in *In re Lifschutz* (1970) a psychiatrist had a client who filed a suit for damages against another party for assault, claiming severe mental and emotional distress. When called for a deposition by the defendant, Dr. Lifschutz refused to answer any questions regarding his client and would not reveal any of the client's records. He maintained that the preservation of confidentiality was more important than the need for the record and that confidentiality was absolute and protected by the privilege. The court disagreed and required that Lifschutz disclose the information.

The obligation of confidentiality is significant for malpractice in two ways. First, it defines an important legal obligation of therapists, and breach of that obligation can lead to malpractice liability. Second, the testimonial privilege associated with confidentiality arises with some frequency in the malpractice area. In this chapter, we review the basic principles of privacy, confidentiality, and privilege and how they work to strike a balance between keeping clients' secrets and protecting the public.

LEGAL PROTECTIONS OF CONFIDENTIALITY

The legal protections of the confidences of therapy arise from many sources: the U.S. Constitution and state constitutions, federal and state statutes and regulations, state licensing laws, codes of ethics, and the common law (developed by courts through case law). For the most part, state law has been of primary importance in protecting confidentiality. Now, however, federal law is becoming more important.

There have been claims that the U.S. Constitution protects some communications in therapy, although any such protection is narrow (Smith, 1986). A number of state constitutions, however, have specific privacy provisions that do provide protections of therapy privacy. The greater protection has come from common law and, more recently, statutes.

The statutes or regulations of many states provide for therapist–client confidentiality and impose damages for the breach of that confidentiality. Even in states in which there is no specific statutory provision creating such liability, it exists by common law or general malpractice or tort principles. The general rules of negligence related to psychologists impose liability for the improper disclosure of such information. Other causes of action (depending on the facts) might also result in liability for the improper release of this information, including breach of contract, intentional infliction of emotional distress, invasion of privacy, and defamation.

The codes of ethics of psychology and all of the major mental health organizations include obligations to protect the confidentiality of clients (e.g., American Association of Marriage and Family Therapists, 2001; APA, 2010; Canadian Psychological Association, 2000; National Association of Social Workers, 2000). The failure to do so may result in disciplinary action by the profession, including the loss of membership in professional organizations. In addition, the licensing laws for the therapy professions have similar ethical standards regarding confidentiality. Violating these obligations may result in the loss or suspension of the license to practice or other penalties.

Federal law is playing an increasingly large role in protecting the privacy of therapy. Some laws provide specific protection for specific kinds of therapy. For example, drug and alcohol treatment programs that are part of federal programs have special and very strict privacy rules (Confidentiality of Alcohol and Drug Abuse Patient Records, 2010; Roth, 2009). Treatment in Veterans Affairs facilities creates confidentiality obligations, and Medicare and Medicaid reimbursement statutes also provide some protections for health information (Hixson, 2005). In recent years, a major federal law, the Health Insurance Portability and Accountability Act of 1996 (HIPAA) has changed the landscape of client information.

The right of confidentiality in therapy communications is intended to protect the client. Thus, the client "owns" the right of confidentiality, and the client may choose to waive, or give up, the confidentiality. Unless the law creates an exception (and there are a number of such exceptions), a therapist may not independently decide to waive confidentiality without the client's consent. At the same time, when clients request copies of their own information, the therapist is usually obligated to release the information.

HEALTH INSURANCE PORTABILITY AND ACCOUNTABILITY ACT

Of all of the recent developments in health care information protection, none is more important than HIPAA. It promises to be a major part of protecting therapy information in the future.

HIPAA, passed in 1996, created protection of electronic records almost as an afterthought. It provided that if Congress did not adopt privacy rules for health information, federal agencies could do so by regulation. Congress did not, and over the years a series of complex HIPAA regulations were developed related to most health records. The HIPAA Privacy Rule was implemented in 2003 (HIPAA Privacy Rule, 2010). In 2009, as part of an economic stimulus bill, Congress adopted the Health Information Technology for Economic and Clinical Health Act (HITECH), which substantially modified and expanded HIPAA obligations. HIPAA and the changes to it under HITECH are too complex to cover adequately in this book. Therefore, in this chapter we focus on the more important issues under the HIPAA Privacy Rule. Psychologists who maintain or transmit client records or information electronically should also comply with the HIPAA Security Rule (2010). Considerable information on HIPAA compliance for psychologists can be found on the APA Practice Organization website (http://www.apapracticecentral.org/business/hipaa/index.aspx).

In a broad sense, HIPAA protects the confidentiality of health records by limiting significantly the release of these records without client consent and by allowing clients to see their own records. In addition, HIPAA provides for informing clients about the confidentiality of their health information and who has had access to that information. The HITECH amendments also provide for notification to clients when health information has been released or "hacked" by third parties (Wachler & Fehn, 2009).

HIPAA generally reinforces state privacy laws and supplements them. Where HIPAA and state health information privacy laws conflict, the one that is more protective of privacy, or that gives clients greater access to their own records, will prevail. Thus, state law will extend beyond HIPAA requirements if the state law provides greater protection for the client's privacy. States are not uniform in their laws governing client access to records; the laws protecting client records vary in application from state to state.

HIPAA recognizes the special sensitivity of psychotherapy records. The law creates two kinds of records: (a) regular treatment records and (b) psychotherapy notes. HIPAA regulations define five criteria pertaining to psychotherapy notes: They must be (a) notes recorded in any medium; (b) by a health care provider who is a mental health professional; (c) documenting or analyzing the contents of a conversation (d) during a private counseling session or a group, joint, or family counseling session; and (e) that are separated from the rest of the individual's record (HIPAA Privacy Rule, 2010). The key is that these notes must analyze or document therapy sessions and be kept separate from the rest of the record (DeLettre & Carter, 2010). Psychotherapy notes do not include records dealing with medication management; start and stop times of therapy sessions; frequencies and modalities of treatment; results of clinical tests; and summaries regarding diagnosis, functional status, treatment plan, prognosis, and progress made in treatment (HIPAA Privacy Rule, 2010). A therapist is allowed, but not required, to keep separate psychotherapy notes.

Psychotherapy notes receive very special treatment under HIPAA. They are not considered part of the regular medical record that can readily be transferred to other professionals. Except in very limited circumstances, even insurance companies may not see psychotherapy notes or withhold payment to force the client to authorize release of the notes (HIPAA Privacy Rule, 2010).

HIPAA limits the transfer of health records to third parties. Such records may be disclosed in certain limited circumstances, where there is consent, or to other health care providers when that is necessary for the continuity of care. Even where a client has consented to the release, the party receiving the information under HIPAA may have an *extended privacy* obligation not to release further the information.

Psychologists face several issues before deciding on a course of action regarding providing third parties access to records. There is first the question of whether the therapist is covered by the HIPAA Privacy Rule (APA

Practice Organization, 2009). Although some psychologists claim that their practice is exempt for one reason or another, this is increasingly unlikely and very risky, given the breadth of HIPAA regulations. We recommend, for a variety of reasons, that all practitioners become HIPAA compliant. When the state in which the therapist practices has provisions in state laws that are more protective of client privacy, then practitioners should follow the more stringent state law because it is presumably more protective of a client's records than is the HIPAA Privacy Rule (APA Practice Organization, 2009).

Some professionals have argued that forensic evaluations are not protected health information and that HIPAA does not apply at all. In fact, the HIPAA Privacy Rule recognizes that court-ordered evaluations and the like are not entirely confidential, given appropriate notice and consent. That does not mean that a forensic psychologist need not have an office and practice that are HIPAA compliant. As a general rule, if there is any HIPAA-covered record in the practice, then the entire practice must be HIPAA compliant (HIPAA Privacy Rule, 2010; Koocher & Connell, 2003).

Another important provision of HIPAA generally allows clients to see their own records. A number of state laws have similar provisions. Ordinarily, the therapist will be obligated under these laws to provide the requested information, but this raises some special problems. Those records that meet the definition of psychotherapy notes, including being separated from the rest of the client's files, are not subject to mandatory disclosure to the client in many states.

This area may become even more complex when clients request their personal health information and the professional believes that release of the records will cause harm to the client or may impede the progress of the treatment. A related issue is whether the client has the legal capacity (competence) to demand that the records be released. In some states a therapist may withhold psychotherapy notes on the basis of therapeutic or mental harm to the client. To withhold personal health information, however, there ordinarily must be the risk of physical harm. The extent to which a therapist can deny clients access to records in such circumstances depends on the interaction among the HIPAA Privacy Rule, state law, and the nature of the records sought.

When withholding information because it is likely to be harmful, the client may still be able to direct the release of the information to a third party. This third party can be an attorney, another mental health care provider, or even a friend.

The APA Ethics Code allows for the withholding of records in circumstances under which the clinician believes that release of the records can cause serious harm. In such circumstances it would be critical to carefully document the therapist's reasons for believing that harm would come from the disclosure. Provisions of state law differ regarding who must carry the burden in these cases, that is, whether the client (or his or her representative) has to demonstrate good cause for disclosure or whether the practitioner bears the burden of proving that disclosure would be harmful.

When the information about the client is entangled with private information about others (e.g., in group or couples therapy), the therapist should not release that information without joint consent or without redacting it so that no information about other clients is disclosed. The APA (2007) Record Keeping Guidelines provide some guidance here, suggesting that when multiple clients are involved the psychologist should consider keeping multiple records, one for each member of the group or the family. Standards 10.02 and 10.03 of the APA Ethics Code describe the necessity of identifying in advance who the client is or clients are; who is viewed as collateral to the treatment; and who will need to sign record releases, should the need arise in the future. This should be part of the informed consent obtained at the outset of treatment.

The HITECH amendments to HIPAA, among other things, generally require that clients be informed when there is an accidental release of health care information by a provider. The amendments permit clients to request from health providers a list of every release of information over a period of years. They also clarify and strengthen the penalties and potential private civil actions for violations of HIPAA (Wachler & Fehn, 2009). Failure to follow the requirements of HIPAA may result in civil penalties, liability, and (in extreme cases) criminal penalties. (APA provides a good overview of HIPAA requirements at http://www.apapracticecentral.org/business/hipaa/2009-privacy.pdf.)

HIPAA and similar state obligations are complicated (Conn, 2009). This is one area in which it is especially important that therapists obtain solid legal advice to stay within the obligations of the law. HIPAA raises a series of complex issues, and practitioners need to be prepared ahead of time with a checklist of relevant considerations or other appropriate guidance in order to make an appropriate response, for instance, to a client's request for access to records.

EXCEPTIONS TO CONFIDENTIALITY

Confidentiality in psychotherapy has many exceptions. Some exceptions are mandatory, in which case the therapist is required to release information. Others are discretionary, in which case the therapist may release information but is not required to do so. Most of the exceptions we discuss in this section are mandatory. We do not deal with every possible exception to confidentiality, only with the major exceptions. For example, in most states a therapist may, without violating confidentiality, consult with another professional for the purpose of receiving assistance or advice related to the care of a client, and many institutions have a quality-improvement process that may include examination of client files.

Consent to the Release of Information

Because the right of confidentiality of psychotherapy belongs to the client, a competent client may waive the confidentiality. The waiver is most often for a limited purpose. A typical waiver, for example, is to obtain reimbursement for services or to transmit information to another health care provider. Therapists are ordinarily obligated to respect the limitations on clients' demands regarding the disclosure of private information. Therefore, the fact that a client has directed the release of specific information does not give a therapist broad authority to release all information. Discussing the disclosure and the extent of the disclosure with the client prior to releasing any information, and confirming this in writing, is a good caution to observe.

HIPAA has imposed several limitations on the release of information subject to the consent of the client. For example, information transmitted to a third party (e.g., an insurance company) that is subject to HIPAA has a form of extended confidentiality in which that third party is precluded from retransmitting the confidential information without additional consent from the client. On the other hand, HIPAA does *not* always require consent for the release of information; for example, it would not be required when child abuse needs to be reported to authorities.

A potential problem arises when a client consents to the release of records that may include copyrighted tests or scoring instructions that could result in a loss of test security. The release of raw psychological test data has been a matter of controversy among psychologists and between the law and psychology. Lees-Haley and Courtney (2000) argued that there is no basis legally or ethically for withholding raw psychological test data from attorneys. Many psychologists disagree with this position.

Lawyers who demand access to such raw data as an essential part of legal discovery argue that they are entitled to anything on which the psychologist has based her or his opinion. Psychologists argue that, to protect the data from misuse, they should provide it only to another psychologist. In the Statement on the Disclosure of Test Data (APA Committee on Psychological Tests and Assessment, 1996) and in "Strategies for Private Practitioners Coping With Subpoenas or Compelled Testimony for Client Records and Test Data" (APA Committee on Legal Issues, 2006), APA has laid out conditions for withholding raw data.

Erard (2004) discussed the difficulties inherent in the 2002 APA Ethics Code. The current APA Ethics Code recognizes the obligation to provide clients copies of their records (see especially Standard 9.04, "Release of Test Data"). Nevertheless, in the case of raw psychological test data a psychologist still may seek to turn them over only to people qualified to interpret them under the theory that not doing so could, in fact, cause substantial harm to the client or result in the misuse of the data. In a related matter, Bennett et al. (2006) discussed the ability to withhold test materials as legally protected trade secrets. These authors suggested either whiting out the test questions or merely sending a list of answers to the client if it is she or he who has requested them. A mental health professional may offer to send test data to another psychologist of the client's choosing or (when release of the test seems inappropriate) request that there be a court order, rather than merely a subpoena, before releasing test records (Behnke, 2004).

In complying with a client's request to transmit information about therapy to third parties, mental health professionals should take a minimalist approach and transmit the minimum necessary to accomplish the client's purpose. Additional information can always be provided if necessary but, once released, information is usually impossible to recapture. This approach would be modified, of course, when the information is being transferred to other health care providers who need the information to diagnose or treat the client.

Dangerous Clients

Many states now require that therapists take reasonable steps to avoid serious harm or death to identifiable potential victims of dangerous clients (Rogge, 2000). In those states, of course, therapists are not only permitted but also may be legally required to breach client confidentiality to avoid harm. We discuss this *Tarasoff* principle in greater detail in Chapter 6.

It is likely that even when the duty to protect is not triggered as a legal requirement—for example, in those circumstances in which there are real (but not identifiable) victims—therapists are permitted to breach confidentiality in order to avoid serious harm. The extent of such a voluntary right, which exists by statute in a number of states, is not always clearly defined. For example, it is not clear how serious the potential harm must be. A therapist who in good faith honestly discloses limited information in order to avoid serious physical harm is generally taking the lesser risk of two evils: serious physical harm versus a violation of confidence. Nevertheless, this is a high-risk situation and, if time and circumstances permit, the therapist should consult with a legal advisor or malpractice insurance carrier. The clinician should consider explaining to the client, perhaps as part of informed consent, that if she or he threatens a third party the therapist may break confidentiality in order to protect that third party.

Child and Other Abuse Reporting Laws

All states have child abuse reporting laws, and most have laws that require reporting of other forms of abuse, such as spouse abuse or abuse of individuals who are elderly and/or disabled (Guedj, Sastre, Mullet, & Scorum, 2009). These laws typically require health care providers to report known or suspected abuse. *Abuse* in this context often includes physical, mental, or sexual abuse, or neglect. Failure to report as required may subject a therapist to civil liability, license discipline, or even criminal charges (Kalichman, 1999); however, the failure to report infrequently results in such liability. Good faith reporting is generally immune from liability (*Marks v. Tenbrunsel,* 2005).

State laws vary somewhat on *who* is obligated to report suspected or known abuse. Some states place the obligation only on those treating or caring for the individual. Other states require "any person" or "professional" who knows or suspects abuse to report the situation. In those states, a mental health professional treating a client who, for example, reveals that he or she is seeking therapy because he or she needs help to stop abusing a child must report the abuse.

When reporting is required, the therapist does not have the latitude to decide that she or he would rather provide treatment to a client than to report the situation. Reporting is mandatory. The therapist should document decisions regarding required reporting. It is also good practice to communicate to clients, as part of informed consent, that the therapist is obligated to make reports of the abuse of children and others. A misunderstanding of this issue is seen in the following example.

Dr. P was consulted by a client who asked Dr. P if everything he said would be confidential. Dr. P said that it would be unless he felt that the client was dangerous. The client then confided in Dr. P that he had been having sexual relations with his 14-year-old daughter. Dr. P made the mandated report to the Department of Social Services. On the basis of this report, the man was arrested and prosecuted for child abuse. He then filed a complaint against Dr. P alleging breach of confidentiality. The breach of confidentiality, of course, was justified, but the confusion arose from Dr. P's failure to inform his client that he had a mandate to report instances of child abuse. His statement about "dangerousness" was vague.

Because all states require that known or suspected child abuse be reported but vary in details of exactly what must be reported, it is important for therapists to review the relevant statutes in their states and to have a specific plan for dealing with known or suspected abuse. In addition, most states have other mandatory reporting statutes (e.g., regarding abuse of individuals who are elderly or have disabilities), and therapists need to be clear on their obligations under those laws. It is helpful to have the guidance of an attorney who is familiar with the state laws. Practitioners may also receive helpful advice from state psychological associations or their malpractice insurance carrier.

Forensic Issues

In forensic cases there is usually an expected communication to a third party, and confidentiality is thus limited. It may not be obvious to the examinee that confidentiality will be limited, however, and that person must have a clear understanding of the expectations of confidentiality before an interview begins. Such an understanding is also important regarding the relationships among the psychologist, attorneys, and the court. Examples of the critical questions are the following: Who is the client? Who will receive the report? Will the report be admissible in evidence and the psychologist required to testify? The answers to these questions will vary from one forensic setting to another, and they need to be clarified, preferably in writing, before any work begins. Standard 3.05 of the APA Ethics Code discusses in detail the issues pertaining to multiple relationships in which psychologists must take on more than one role.

The limits of confidentiality should be spelled out and included in the informed consent to avoid any misunderstanding by the examinee or others who may be involved in the legal proceeding. These limits will vary from, say, a criminal competency case to a child custody evaluation (Benjamin, Andrew, & Gollan, 2003). In some forensic cases the psychologist may be appointed by the court as a "neutral" expert. More frequently, one party or the other may engage the psychologist. In any event, everyone should understand the rules before consultation begins (Rogers & Shuman, 2005).

When engaged by one party to conduct an examination, the psychologist is not part of that "side" in terms of becoming an advocate (S. R. Smith, 1989). The Specialty Guidelines for Forensic Psychologists (APA Committee on Ethical Guidelines for Forensic Psychologists, 1991) describe the necessity for forensic psychologists to approach a case from all reasonable perspectives and actively seek out data that will test competing rival hypotheses. Once psychologists have objectively reviewed all such data and reached conclusions based on the data, they may present and defend their findings. This constitutes being an advocate for the professional opinion, not for one side or the other.

The lack of the usual expectations of confidentiality in a forensic case does not mean that there is a freedom to do whatever the psychologist wishes with information obtained in that setting. Indeed, there may be multiple legal and ethical obligations regarding confidentiality. The examinee's identity and information are not necessarily public, and it would not be appropriate for the psychologist to unilaterally decide to make them so. The psychologist may also owe duties of confidentiality to the attorney representing one side or the other, or to the court. The person or persons to whom a forensic report may be released will depend on the circumstances (e.g., who is engaging the psychologist, the purposes of the report, and the rules of evidence). It is therefore important that forensic experts have a clear understanding at the time they are engaged as an expert regarding the release and distribution of the report. The attorney or court appointing the expert should be willing to provide this information. In general, psychologists working in the role of forensic expert should be reluctant to disclose material until it is clearly permissible to do so.

CONSEQUENCES OF BREACHES OF CONFIDENTIALITY

Most courts recognize a breach of confidence as negligence. Some states also allow invasion of privacy (disclosure of private facts without authority) and breach of contract (based on a broken promise of secrecy) as the bases for recovery (S. R. Smith, 1991). The release of false or misleading information may be defamation or the privacy tort of *false light*.

The extent to which a therapist may disclose information is limited by the breadth of the client's consent. For example, if a client were to sign a waiver to an insurance company so that the therapist can be paid, this is a partial consent to the release of information. It does not, however, allow unfettered disclosure of that information by the therapist. The therapist cannot, on the basis of such a waiver, therefore, write a book about the client's therapy. The case of *Doe v. Roe* (1977) illustrates the importance of written waivers of confidentiality and that therapists should exercise the greatest caution when a waiver will not directly benefit the client. In this case, the court held that the client's oral waiver of confidentiality obtained during treatment was not valid for the therapist to describe the client's condition and treatment as part of a book. Any practitioner contemplating publishing information from therapy must not only document the consent given by the client but also make sure that the client is competent to give such consent. HIPAA reinforces this ethical and common law principle that disclosure by client consent is limited to that permitted by the client.

The importance of therapists understanding the obligations of confidentiality, exercising reasonable professional judgment, and documenting decisions related to the release of information is illustrated by the following example case, in which a therapist was seeing a woman in psychotherapy who would frequently vent her frustration about her work in her sessions. At times these ventings contained some threats to harm certain individuals; however, on the basis of a careful assessment the therapist evaluated this as "blowing off steam," did not take the threats seriously, and felt no need to take protective measures. His records documented the fact that these threats were never accompanied by any acting out. On one occasion, the client told her therapist that if people at work did not stop harassing her, she was going to blow up the factory. Although the client had made similar empty threats, on this occasion the therapist chose to break the confidentiality and notify people at the factory of the woman's threats. Of note is the fact that there was nothing in the therapist's records that indicated why the therapist regarded this statement—which was no different from any of the previously threatening but ultimately harmless statements, or from any subsequent statements—as a credible threat. In this instance the therapist did not document the clinical judgment that led to releasing confidential communication. The woman was fired, and she filed suit against the therapist for breach of confidentiality.

A notable instance involving confidentiality was that of the poet Anne Sexton, who before her death had been in therapy with psychiatrist Dr. Martin Orne (Orne 1991). Orne made 300 therapy tapes available to Diane Wood Middlebrook, who was writing a biography of Sexton. Sexton had never given Orne any explicit written consent to release the tapes, although Orne did have the permission of Sexton's daughter and literary executor to let Middlebrook hear the tapes. (The release of confidential therapy information following the death of the client is most commonly determined by the *executor*, the person left to manage the estate of the client.) Orne's release of the tapes created a firestorm of controversy. He was condemned as betraying his profession and his client for choosing to release the tapes, even though he was probably legally permitted to do so.

Behnke, Winick, and Perez (1999, pp. 146–149) presented very helpful suggestions for what a therapist needs to do under circumstances relating to confidentiality of the records of deceased clients. The suggestions include obtaining prior written authorization from the client for release of materials; an analysis of what the client would have wanted if he or she did not give explicit written consent; and a consideration of whether there were other, less intrusive means of obtaining the same information.

The HIPAA Privacy Rule, as modified by HITECH, sets forth minimum standards for confidentiality on a nationwide basis, as we described in greater detail earlier in this chapter. Also as noted earlier, some state laws regarding protection of confidential client information are more protective of privacy than HIPAA. Violation of these state privacy laws can create the potential for civil liability.

Although most therapists are scrupulous about protecting confidential information, accidental breaches do occur. Conversations about a client at a business meeting, at a restaurant, or on a voicemail left on an answering machine that may be accessed by people other than the intended person can be problematic. In addition, computer records may be inadvertently released or stolen. These are unintentional breaches of confidentiality, and therapists need to be very careful to avoid them. (HIPAA also has a security rule that applies to computer records and the electronic transmission of records. These regulations are complex and generally require professional advice to implement.) Some of these accidental disclosures now, under HITECH, have more serious ramifications. In some instances clients will have to be informed of accidental disclosure, and reports of some accidental disclosures must be transmitted to federal agencies and placed on providers' websites (HITECH, 2009).

Among the most unusual consequences of breach of confidentiality have been securities violations: In *United States v. Willis* (1990), two mental health professionals were charged with insider trading for using secret business information revealed in therapy to engage in stock trading (Nash, 1986).

It is likely that only a very small proportion of the possible lawsuits for breach of confidentiality are ever filed. For many reasons, clients are reluctant to file these claims. Among other things, the claims are public, and clients thus risk even greater losses of confidentiality by bringing a public lawsuit. In most cases the damages (financial, emotional, or reputational) are not great or are at least speculative and hard to prove. On the other hand, a particularly sympathetic plaintiff, or especially outrageous conduct by the defendant, may result in significant damages. Beyond litigation, however, unhappy clients may file complaints with state licensing boards, professional associations, or the federal government (i.e., regarding HIPAA).

PRACTICAL SUGGESTIONS

1. Client privacy and confidentiality are among the most important professional values for psychologists. In addition to their ethical commitment to client privacy, therapists should know that the law imposes damages for the breach of that confidentiality. Most commonly, breach of confidentiality is considered negligence, but other possible causes of action include breach of contract, invasion of privacy, and defamation.

2. The right of confidentiality in therapy communications is intended to protect the client. The client, not the therapist, "owns" the right of confidentiality, and the client may choose to waive the confidential-

ity. Psychologists should convey these limits to their clients in a carefully crafted informed consent document.

3. Therapists need to be familiar with a major federal law, HIPAA (as amended by HITECH), that has changed the landscape of client information. HIPAA protects confidentiality of health records by significantly limiting the release of these records without client consent and by allowing clients to see their own records. The law provides special protection to psychotherapy notes.

4. Therapists need to understand the laws of their states as well as HIPAA. When the HIPAA Privacy Rule and state health information privacy laws conflict, the one that is more protective of privacy or gives clients greater access to their records will prevail.

5. Therapists need to be HIPAA compliant—not an easy task. HIPAA and similar state obligations are complicated. This is one area in which it is especially important that therapists obtain solid legal advice to stay within the obligations of the law.

6. Clients may waive confidentiality and direct therapists to release information from therapy. Such releases are generally for a limited purpose, and therapists should release the information only to the extent to which they are directed to do so. Discussing the disclosure and the extent of the disclosure with the client prior to release is a good caution to observe.

7. Clients may request to see their own records, and ordinarily therapists should comply with the request. When that could harm the client or result in the violation of testing copyright protection or trade secrets, or when state law allows withholding psychotherapy notes, the therapist may withhold some information.

8. Psychologists should have a process in place to ensure that reports of child or other abuse are made consistent with state law. Therapists are legally obligated to report known or suspected child abuse as defined by state law. Some states require other abuse reporting.

9. In forensic evaluations the limits of confidentiality must be spelled out and included in the informed consent to avoid any misunderstanding by the examinee or others potentially involved in the legal proceeding.

5

Negligent Diagnosis and Treatment

An incorrect diagnosis is not necessarily a negligent diagnosis. Mistakes may be nonnegligent, in that they were carefully arrived at and professionally acceptable. In addition, competent practitioners with different theoretical orientations may differ in their diagnosis of a given client. For example, a psychologist with a psychodynamic orientation may well choose to emphasize different aspects of the client's presentation than would a psychologist with a cognitive behavioral orientation. As we noted in Chapter 2, the law recognizes schools of thought in health care and will generally hold practitioners to the standard of care of a reputable school of thought to which they subscribe.

Although most practitioners currently use the *Diagnostic and Statistical Manual of Mental Disorders* (4th ed., text revision; *DSM–IV–TR;* American Psychiatric Association, 2000), there is some controversy regarding the validity and reliability of the diagnoses, the lack of hard science in them, the proliferation of disorders, the lack of causation or explanatory material, and the unjustified categorical distinction between disorders (Chodoff, 2005; Kendell & Jablonsky, 2003; Pincus, Zarin, & First, 1998). Some equally well-trained practitioners are now using *The Psychodynamic Diagnostic*

Manual of the Alliance of Psychodynamic Organizations (2006), which represents the collaborative efforts of several psychoanalytically based organizations and deals more with underlying causes of behavior, as opposed to the symptoms that form the basis of *DSM–IV–TR*. As of this printing, a draft of *DSM–V* has been released for comment and has resulted in similar controversies revolving around diagnoses with questionable validity, such as parental alienation syndrome and paraphilic coercive disorder.

In this chapter, we look in more detail at what negligence means in the context of psychological diagnosis and treatment.

NEGLIGENT DIAGNOSIS

Courts are fairly flexible in applying standards of care in psychological diagnosis because of the inherent ambiguities of these diagnoses. Instead of the incorrect diagnosis being the focus, then, the central point is often the *reason* that the diagnosis was faulty. Malpractice liability is most likely when the psychologist deviated from accepted standards in performing a diagnostic assessment or negligently missed the appropriate diagnosis because of inattention or careless interpretation of the assessment. Hunches or guesses unsupported by solid psychometric workups are not justified as clinical practice. They are not supported by ethical guidelines or professional practice standards and likely constitute malpractice.

In one recent instance, a woman presented herself for treatment to a therapist complaining of depression, headaches, dizziness, and some periods which she described as "losing time." The psychologist's diagnostic assessment consisted of the Rorschach (Exner, 2002), Minnesota Multiphasic Personality Inventory—2 (MMPI–2; Tellegen, Dahlstrom, Butcher, & Graham, 2001), and Bender Visual–Motor Gestalt Test (Bender, 2003). Not surprisingly, the MMPI–2 and the Rorschach were consistent with diagnoses of anxiety and depression. The psychologist considered, but rejected, possible brain impairment as contributing to the symptoms, because the Bender–Gestalt results were within normal limits. The use of the Bender–Gestalt as a screening instrument for brain damage has been superseded in the last 30 years by a variety of more sophisticated neuropsychological instruments (Bigler, 1981). Relying on the Bender–Gestalt to rule out brain impairment is a very risky procedure because the vast major-ity of current professional literature describes such screenings as inappro-priate (Bigler, 1981). Were any of the client's symptoms, in fact, due to an undiagnosed brain impairment, and she were to develop a neurological ill-ness, the psychologist could have been professionally liable for negligent diagnosis. In fact, it is essential, according to the *DSM–IV–TR,* to rule out the contribution to presenting symptoms of a general medical condition or substance abuse. Because this cannot be done by a psychologist, it is fre-quently necessary to obtain a medical consultation.

The Council of Representatives of the American Psychological Asso-ciation (APA) recently supported a move to work on the most recent edi-tion (11th) of the *International Classification of Diseases and Related Health Problems,* which, as of this printing, is in development by the World Health Organization. This would provide an alternative diagnostic system to the upcoming *DSM–V.*

Hedges (2007) noted the need to demonstrate adherence to a sound diagnostic assessment procedure. He suggested five components to this: (a) making a diagnosis, (b) documenting it in the client's file, (c) using the diagnosis in formulations and in contact with third parties, (d) sharing it with the client, and (e) periodically updating it.

Ted Blackwell's case against Kaiser Permanente (2007; Perkes, 2007) illustrates the consequences of inadequate diagnosis. Doctors diagnosed Ted Blackwell's headaches as being caused by a grief reaction to the death of his brother and refused to order a computed tomography scan, believ-ing that it was not necessary despite Blackwell's daughter's descriptions of his continued headaches and disorientation. As a result, Blackwell's brain aneurysm was not diagnosed, and he suffered cerebral bleeding and permanent brain damage. Damages of $1.8 million were awarded in arbitration.

Psychologists need to be careful in their diagnoses and base them only on examinations that are sufficiently thorough to justify any diag-nosis. In *Russell v. Adams* (1997), the plaintiff contended that the defen-dant, Dr. Adams, had caused her to become alienated from her daughter. The daughter was Adams's client, and Adams had diagnosed the mother as mentally ill and abusive, with borderline personality characteristics.

This diagnosis was not accurate, but on its basis Adams recommended that the daughter cut off all ties to the mother. This case highlights the necessity for extreme caution in making diagnoses. The claim was dismissed by the court because Adams did not owe a duty to the mother, who was not a client.

Consistent with the APA's (2010) "Ethical Principles of Psychologists and Code of Conduct," a psychologist should make a diagnosis only when there is sufficient information to back it up. A mere feeling, intuition, or guess that someone fits a diagnostic category should not be the basis for a diagnosis. The practitioner needs to be able to detail which diagnostic criteria went into the formulation of the diagnosis. The doctor in *Russell v. Adams* (1997) created a faulty diagnosis of Mrs. Russell (the mother) because he apparently had not seen her in therapy. If what is purportedly a diagnosis is actually some discussion between the therapist and the client, then the therapist needs to make very clear that this is not a diagnosis, avoid making recommendations based on the "diagnosis," and document all of that in the records.

When psychological tests are given, they must be administered, scored, and interpreted according to standard procedures. Innovative interpretations of tests that are not consistent with accepted interpretations must be avoided; furthermore, any reservations regarding the validity or reliability of the interpretation due to certain situational factors or differences of the client from the norm group need to be documented. Consider the following examples.

Dr. H was counseling a couple and wanted to emphasize to the wife that she had difficulty getting close to men because of some difficulties in her relationship with her father. He told her that her MMPI–2 profile peaked on the scale that measures distrust of men. There is, of course, no such scale on this test, and his attempt to make a point involved a clear example of diagnostic negligence.

Another example of the misuse of an MMPI–2 profile was by a psychologist who claimed that on the basis of such a profile he could tell who was lying when clients said that they did not sexually abuse their children. He described this scale as the "only psychological test measure there is of lying." Once again, of course, there is no such scale on the MMPI–2. The psychologist in question was using elevations on the L scale, which measures outright denial of any faults or foibles to which most people readily admit (e.g., "Once in awhile I laugh at a dirty joke"), to justify his statements. This scale tends to be elevated in many individuals engaged in custody situations, who may be presenting an overly virtuous picture of themselves. To describe the L scale as one that measures lying when there are allegations of child abuse involved is certainly a misrepresentation and an example of diagnostic negligence.

Early critiques of the Rorschach test noted that it was highly subjective and depended for the most part on the psychologist doing the interpreting. This has largely changed since the availability of Exner's Comprehensive System (Exner, 1993), which has extensive empirical support. Nowadays, clinicians who do not score the Rorschach but instead intuitively or subjectively interpret it are deviating from accepted practice. In a similar manner, psychologists who do not administer the whole test along with an inquiry, but instead do a "quick screen," also are generally departing from standard practice.

In one example of diagnostic negligence, a psychologist evaluated a client before the client underwent elective surgery that was somewhat experimental. As part of the informed consent procedure, clients seeking the surgery had to have a psychological evaluation to determine that they did not suffer from any significant mental illnesses that might be a contraindication to the surgery. The psychologist administered a Rorschach but did not score it and concluded that the client did not have any mental illness. When the client was ultimately dissatisfied with the surgery and filed suit, the fact that the psychologist based an opinion on a Rorschach that was not scored resulted in a finding of professional negligence. The plaintiff retained the services of a psychologist who did score the Rorschach protocols and found many examples of "special scores" that were consistent with a psychotic disorder.

Mental health professionals also must be exceedingly careful in their use of and reference to certain conditions and syndromes that lack empirical support. Not only is this risky as far as potential liability goes, it also represents a violation of several standards according to APA. The APA Ethics Code cautions psychologists to rely on established knowledge of the field and make conclusions only when they have sufficient data to back up the claim.

Two areas that have been problematic stem from the late Dr. Richard Gardner's work dealing with sexual abuse allegations. Gardner created an instrument that he maintained could differentiate real from fabricated instances of child sexual abuse. There have never been any empirical studies performed to test this instrument or to demonstrate the pervasiveness—or, for that matter, the existence—of what Gardner termed *parental alienation syndrome* (Gardner, 1992). Nevertheless, it assumed somewhat of an urban legend quality. Courts would order parental alienation syndrome evaluations, and many mental health professionals would use this terminology in their reports (Bruch, 2001). APA went so far as to caution against the diagnosis of this "syndrome" by professional psychologists, noting that there is no scientific evidence for its existence (APA, 1996). Some other examples of syndromes that lack empirical evidence are false memory syndrome and malicious mother syndrome (*Wiederholt v. Fischer*, 1992; Pope, 1996; Turkat, 1995).

In short, mental health professionals may be subject to malpractice liability if they fail to adequately test or diagnose a client and such failure causes harm. The examination itself may be conducted in a negligent manner, or the psychologist may not understand the nature, proper use, or limitations of a test. Drawing far-reaching conclusions that cannot be justified on the basis of the literature surrounding a particular test also puts the therapist at risk for malpractice. Examples of this are stating that a particular MMPI–2 profile is normative for a child molester or that the results of the Rorschach demonstrate that a particular client could not have committed a certain crime.

The risk of malpractice in forensic psychology is probably lower than in other areas of practice, but it does not disappear altogether. Significant ethical issues arise in this area. Problems in forensic diagnosis mirror the careless practices noted throughout this chapter: failing to conduct adequate examinations and assessments, misapplying or misinterpreting tests, not using standard scoring of instruments, and using hunches or guesses to replace good clinical practice (Goldstein, 2003).

Special problems of diagnosis can arise in forensic arenas. One is confusion of the roles of expert witness, therapist, decision-maker, and legal expert (Bowermaster, 2002). Although there are some exceptions, in general therapists should render opinions only on the course of treatment, including such matters as diagnosis, prognosis, and the nature of the condition being treated. They should not attempt to answer questions regarding psycholegal issues, such as whether the automobile accident was the proximate cause of the anxiety for which the client was seeking treatment. To answer this question, the practitioner would have to understand the complex legal tests for *proximate cause.*

There are also differences between a *treating expert* and a *forensic expert.* A treating expert needs to be especially cautious in offering opinions that go beyond the examination that expert has done. Too often in forensic settings therapists allow themselves to be manipulated into rendering an opinion that is beyond the examination conducted or the expertise of the psychologist. This can be a particular problem for therapists not experienced in forensic work. Ethics committees see such complaints with some frequency. Standard 2.01 of the APA (2010) Ethics Code addresses issues related to the boundaries of psychologists' competence.

A forensic expert may have access to a wider range of records and information beyond the contact with the examinee (e.g., review of prior records, interviews with collateral sources, administration of psychological tests, assessment of malingering) and may offer a different range of opinions. These are matters that a therapist typically would not investigate; in fact, doing such further investigation could well interfere with the therapeutic relationship. Yet these are precisely the matters that forensic evaluators should take into consideration in their assessment.

EMPLOYMENT TESTING

Mental health professionals are frequently involved in the development and validation of psychological tests, including employment and education tests. Bersoff (1981) observed that legal involvement in psychological testing improves the search for better assessment methods, brings racial and cultural biases to public attention, and makes psychologists more aware of the need to act in a responsible manner.

Testing that is defective in design or validation may harm those taking the test as well as those relying on its results. For instance, a test that is shown to discriminate against female applicants in an employment setting could result in unfair discrimination and liability for the company and the test developer.

Employment screening or testing raises the risk of violation of various civil rights laws if the screening intentionally or incidentally (without legal justification) discriminates against groups that have particular legal protection. Various federal and state civil rights laws prohibit discrimination, for example, on the basis of race, gender, age, or disability. Such discrimination also may result in liability.

Intentional discrimination occurs when the test is used with the purpose of disadvantaging or harming a group or when it is clearly going to disadvantage members of that group without a legitimate business or educational purpose. Another form of discrimination may occur when a test or screening device is used that has a *disparate impact* on protected groups; that is, in its actual operation it disadvantages a group protected by the law (e.g., on the basis of gender or age). This discrimination is not intentional, but it may still give rise to liability under civil rights laws. When there is disparate impact the employer and the psychologist must demonstrate that there is a legitimate business or employment reason for using the test. For example, if an employment test eliminated women from an applicant pool at a much higher rate than men, the psychologist responsible for test administration and scoring needs to demonstrate that there is a legitimate job-related reason for the difference and that there is not another adequate, nondiscriminatory test available. Suppose that the difference occurs because the test uses hypothetical situations based on football. The difference might be justified if the position is for a college sports announcer but not if it is for a retail store clerk.

In the employment context, psychologists must always be aware of the potential for non–job-related disparate impact in constructing, selecting, scoring, and using tests and other screening devices. The validity and relia-bility of the test or screening for the particular position are very important to establish.

An area that is becoming increasingly problematic for psychologists in preemployment screenings and testing is related to the Americans With Disabilities Act of 1990 (ADA), which, among other things, prohibits dis-crimination in the hiring and employment screenings of persons with disabilities, either physical or mental. ADA was amended in 2008 to expand the reach of the law, in particular in employment (Long, 2008). ADA also applies to educational testing and screening. In this chapter, we can provide only the briefest highlights of ADA issues, but any psychologist working in the employment or education testing areas must become familiar with the details of these laws.

ADA—and, to a lesser degree the Rehabilitation Act of 1973—raises issues for psychologists in three ways. These can be especially relevant because some persons with mental illness qualify as disabled under the law. First, psychologists may be asked to screen individuals to determine whether they are qualified to hold a specific position. Tests that intention-ally discriminate or have a disparate impact on persons with disabilities are illegal unless they have a legitimate, job-related basis for assessing that impact. ADA requires that any such qualifications be an essential part of the job and that the person be able to do these essential functions with or without reasonable accommodation. Second, psychologists may be asked to determine what accommodation would be reasonable to permit an employee or applicant to perform the essential functions of a job. Third, ADA has special provisions related to employees who may be dangerous, and psychologists may be called on to determine an applicant's potential for violence in the employment setting.

An employer cannot discriminate against a qualified individual with a disability if the person can basically perform the job with or without reason-able accommodations. This is particularly problematic if the individual has a mental disorder, because the psychologist, during the preemployment screening process, is prohibited from asking questions about the presence of a mental disorder and may not even use a test that is commonly used for the diagnosis of mental disorders. Some courts, for instance, have held that the use of the MMPI–2 (Tellegen et al., 2001) as a preemployment screening instrument may violate ADA (e.g., *Karraker v. Rent-A-Center*, 2005).

When the psychologist believes that a particular applicant's mental disorder may influence employment performance, there is a dilemma. Although personality traits directly related to the job under consideration may be taken into account by the evaluator, usually the mere presence of a mental disorder is not sufficient to deny employment. For example, suppose a potential employee had severe obsessive–compulsive disorder that made him check his work 20 times before submitting it. The disorder itself could not be the basis for disqualifying the applicant, but the inability of the potential employee to perform a particular job with reasonable efficiency might be a legitimate reason for not offering employment. In a similar manner, an applicant for a job as a receptionist/greeter for a building cannot be asked about a past history of a mental condition that, for example, makes him or her severely overreactive to frustration (e.g., intermittent explosive disorder). The practitioner may, however, design a protocol that will reveal the potential for disruptive behavior without asking the client about a preexisting condition or using any tests designed to assist in the diagnosis of mental disorders.

One other area of potential liability in employment testing arises when someone being tested presents with a possible illness that requires rather immediate attention. Although the psychologist may be working for the company considering hiring the examinee, the professional also owes some minimal duty of care to the applicant. Suppose the person being examined suffers from a physical or emotional condition that the psychologist discovers, with the possibility of serious harm or death—for example, is at risk of an imminent stroke. Whether this situation is viewed as involving a quasi-client (in addition to the company being a client) or as an obligation to a third party, there may be some obligation to take action to at least inform the examinee of the finding. This duty is a limited one; that is, the psychologist is not required to conduct a full examination as though the person were coming as a regular client for care but, at a minimum, serious matters discovered in the course of testing should be revealed (or other action taken).

EDUCATIONAL TESTING

Psychologists are also involved in educational testing. Some work to develop educational tests. Many others are involved in accommodations under the ADA and Rehabilitation Act of 1973, and the Individuals With Disabilities Education Improvement Act of 1997 with 2004 Amendments (IDEA). Although all of these acts produce substantial litigation, little of it is malpractice or professional liability directed at psychologists (Parry, 2010). We therefore pause for only a brief summary of educational testing.

The construction and administration of educational testing raise some of the same issues of discrimination that are present in employment testing (e.g., validity, reliability, discrimination, disparate impact). Standardized tests regarding learning disability or educational placement, graduation qualification, academic program admission, or professional licensing raise legal issues. These challenges, however, are ordinarily directed to the test makers, not the psychologists and psychometricians assisting with developing and validating the tests.

Psychologists are also involved with students seeking to have their rights accommodated under ADA or IDEA or state laws that are similar. ADA requires that testing procedures and educational institutions make reasonable accommodations for individuals with disabilities. IDEA requires that public schools, in cooperation with parents, establish acceptable individualized educational plans for students with learning or mental disabilities. Such accommodations and individualized plans are generally based on the opinions and reports of mental health professionals. It is common for universities and testing organizations also to employ mental health professionals to review individual requests for accommodation.

These assessments have not resulted in a lot of malpractice claims against psychologists. Perhaps this is in part because if a student is unhappy with the diagnosis or recommendations of one professional, the student simply seeks an opinion from another. Also, when a student is unhappy with the accommodation offered by the institution (acting on advice of a psychologist, perhaps), the student has several incentives to simply sue the institution instead of the psychologist.

NEGLIGENT TREATMENT

Negligent treatment liability applies most of the same principles as negligent diagnosis. Those basic principles include the following:

- Not all bad outcomes are as a result of negligent treatment.
- In psychotherapy there are many schools of thought regarding the appropriate treatment techniques to be applied to a client or to a condition.
- The psychologist is not responsible for a perfect outcome, but liability may be imposed for adopting unreasonable treatment plans or carelessly applying treatment.
- Therapists must practice only within the bounds of their competency. An example of what not to do is the case of *Hungerford v. Jones* (1998), in which the therapist attended one lecture on memory retrieval techniques at a weekend symposium and regarded this as sufficient training to treat clients with repressed memories of sexual abuse. She allegedly convinced a client that the client had been sexually abused by her father; evidence later revealed that the client had apparently not been abused.
- Where liability does arise, it is often based on negligent diagnosis, or a claim that treatment was not carefully done or applied or is unsupported by a reputable school of thought. Almost any treatment modality can be applied sloppily or without proper supervision.
- It is important to periodically assess the progress of treatment and to modify it as needed.
- Consultations are appropriate when there are therapeutic impasses or difficulties working with a particular client (e.g., countertransference) and when dealing with a high-risk client, such as an individual with borderline personality disorder with a history of suicide attempts (Berman, 2006).

- Referral of some clients to other professionals for treatment sometimes is good professional practice and should not be delayed or avoided.
- Undertaking nontraditional or experimental treatments without proper controls creates a malpractice risk.
- Good record keeping helps reconstruct that a therapist undertook reasonable treatment options for good, sensible reasons.

MANAGED CARE

Managed care creates a number of diagnosis and treatment problems for psychologists. For example, psychologists on managed care panels sometimes find themselves, if not deliberately misdiagnosing, "bending" the diagnosis a bit so that they can get insurance coverage for the treatment of that client (called *up-coding*). A therapist, for example, may diagnose a client with major depression and not diagnose the Axis II condition of borderline personality disorder, fearing that the insurance company will use the Axis II diagnosis as an excuse to not cover the treatment. In a similar manner, a psychologist may diagnose a more serious condition, such as dissociative identity disorder, instead of a more benign one, such as generalized anxiety disorder, feeling that the insurance company will pay for more sessions to treat the more serious diagnosis. Although psychologists may justify this as being able to obtain more treatment for a client in need, it may be seen by the insurance company as a deliberate effort to defraud, especially if the treatment notes do not reflect the more serious diagnosis (Bennett et al., 2006).

Such tinkering with diagnoses can cause legal problems (Hixson, 2005). To the extent that it is dishonest and the therapist benefits from the misstated diagnosis, of course, it may be a form of insurance fraud. It may also create unknown problems for the client in creating an insurance record that could make future life or disability insurance difficult to purchase. In addition, should the diagnosis or treatment of the client ever give rise to a malpractice claim, the incorrect diagnosis, even if done to help the client, will make it look as though the therapist is either incompetent (because the diagnosis is not supported by the record) or dishonest (because the therapist lied to the insurance company to improve reimbursement). Up-coding and the like are dangerous practices, no matter how well intentioned (Appelbaum, 1996).

In the next section, we discuss in detail cases that involved negligent diagnosis and treatment.

CASE ILLUSTRATIONS

Two sad cases from Ohio illustrate very different professional approaches under difficult circumstances. These cases also demonstrate that courts give the mental health professions great, but not unlimited, latitude in diagnosis and treatment.

In *Estates of Morgan v. Fairfield Family Counseling Center* (1997), a client was diagnosed with schizophrenia with pronounced delusional ideas. Several mental health professionals at the mental health center where the client was receiving treatment concurred in the diagnosis, but one of them (who had never read the voluminous records and had not consulted with previous therapists) believed that the client demonstrated signs of malingering. This doctor cut the client's medication in half. The client's condition deteriorated. No referral was made for the client to be reevaluated for a change in medication. His condition continued to deteriorate, and he developed symptoms of a severe paranoid disorder. He was seen by both a psychologist and a vocational counselor. When he subsequently failed to keep an appointment with his therapist, he was seen exclusively by the vocational counselor. Two months later, he was seen by a psychologist, who was of the opinion that he could be neither hospitalized involuntarily nor forced to take medication against his will. Shortly thereafter, the client shot and killed his parents and injured his sister.

He was later found not guilty by reason of insanity, and the estate sued, alleging that the mental health center's negligence was the proximate cause of the parents' deaths and the sister's injuries. The plaintiff's experts testified that there was a substantial deviation from the standard of care in that the doctor negligently failed to make a proper diagnosis, obtain an adequate history, appropriately monitor the client after discontinuation of the medication, review records, and contact his previous treating doctors; discontinued his medication; and improperly delegated care to a vocational counselor. There was testimony that discontinuing medication had a high likelihood of causing a return of the violent behavior.

The Ohio Supreme Court noted that under the "reasonable professional judgment rule," liability could not be imposed on therapists for simple errors in judgment. Instead, the court had to look at whether the psychiatrist's decision was consistent with acceptable practice. Some elements to consider were evidence of thoughtfulness, comprehensiveness of assessment, the competence and training of the therapists involved, whether relevant documents were "promptly and independently reviewed," and whether there was appropriate consultation with other trained and competent professionals. Ultimately, the determination of liability was given to a jury, but the court was critical of the treating psychiatrist for not having reviewed prior records and not having seen the client for approximately 10 months prior to the shooting, even when the parents were complaining about his deteriorating condition. The court also criticized the psychiatrist for being so unaware of the client's condition and for diagnosing the client when there was a documented record of severe psychotic illness in the records (which the doctor did not read). The reasonable professional judgment rule is based on a careful examination of all relevant facts, which the court believed the doctor did not perform.

By contrast, in *Griffin v. Twin Valley Psychiatric System* (2002) the plaintiff claimed that the hospital negligently treated and discharged a former psychiatric client who committed several murders and assaults 4 months after his release. He had been involuntarily committed to the facility and remained there approximately 10 weeks. He was then discharged for further aftercare follow-up. The treatment team consisted of a psychiatrist, a psychologist, a social worker, a group psychotherapist, an activity therapist, and several nursing personnel. There was a well-crafted plan for outpatient follow-up that was put together between the hospital and the outpatient clinic early in the client's hospitalization, and the outpatient case manager met frequently with the client long before his discharge to make advance plans for the outpatient follow-up. The treating psychiatrist requested that the outpatient treatment center place the client in their highest level of case management because of concerns about the severity of the client's condition.

We can already see a sharp distinction between this well-coordinated treatment effort and the rather haphazard approach described in *Estates of Morgan v. Fairfield Family Counseling Center* (1997). This well-considered treatment approach was central to the court's determination that the standard of care was met. Noting the client's history of noncompliance with medication, the hospital, as part of its treatment program, placed the client on a self-medication program to test his compliance. The aftercare agency had the resources and capability of providing intensive case management, psychiatric evaluation and care, medication monitoring, community outreach, psychotherapy, and crisis intervention.

It was rather clear from the well-documented record, the active involvement of many treatment personnel, the coordination of treatment efforts with an aftercare agency, and the extensiveness of the evaluations that the hospital and professionals were conducting their evaluations and delivering treatment consistent with the standard of care. The court relied on criteria that included the competence and training of the therapists, review of relevant documentation and evidence, and adequate professional consultation.

The court in this case repeatedly returned to the premise that liability cannot be imposed simply because of the bad outcome or because a different reasonable treatment approach had not been used. For instance, in this case some of the plaintiff's experts were of the opinion that discharge was inappropriate without trial visits being used first and that not using trial visits initially represented a deviation from the standard of care. The court noted that these are merely differences of professional opinion and could not be the grounds for negligence liability. The issue, according to the court, was whether the method of treatment chosen was consistent with reasonable professional judgment. Finally, the court acknowledged the difficulty of predicting future violent behavior. The court stated that therapists have done their duty if, after examining all the relevant data, they make a reasonable judgment that the client will not harm others. Again, the practitioner need not have chosen a perfect treatment, just an acceptable one.

What can practitioners learn from these cases? Professional judgment is very flexible, but not infinitely so. The basics of good diagnostic work, performed by competent individuals, are always essential; timely evaluations that are comprehensive in nature; consultation, done only by qualified individuals; attention paid to relevant information; and a review of relevant records.

PRACTICAL SUGGESTIONS

1. Perform psychological assessments according to established documented standards. Malpractice liability is most likely when there is failure to conduct adequate examinations and assessments, misapplication or misinterpretation of tests, failure to use standard scoring of instruments, or reliance on hunches or guesses in place of good clinical practice.

2. The five components of sound diagnostic procedures are (a) making a diagnosis, (b) documenting it in the file, (c) using the diagnosis in treatment formulations and in contact with third parties, (d) sharing it with the client, and (e) periodically updating it. Consider the possibility of a physical basis for psychological symptoms.

3. Do not "bend" a diagnosis for managed care. It may be fraudulent and in the long run may do the client more harm than good.

4. In diagnosis or treatment, consultations are appropriate when you encounter therapeutic impasses; difficulties working with a particular client (e.g., countertransference); and high-risk clients, such as an individual with borderline personality disorder with a history of suicide attempts. Document the consultation.

5. In the forensic arena, render opinions only on the course of treatment, including such matters as diagnosis, prognosis, and the nature of the condition being treated. Do not attempt to answer questions regarding psycholegal issues. Treating experts need to be especially cautious in offering opinions that go beyond the examination that expert has done. They should make diagnostic statements only about people they have

personally examined. They should avoid mixing therapeutic and forensic roles.

6. When involved in employment or education testing, be aware of the many legal issues that surround such assessments and tests. Be particularly aware of ADA and IDEA.

7. Practice within the boundaries of your competence; short-term training is insufficient. Consider a period of supervised work when undertaking new therapies.

8. Use only well-validated treatment techniques.

9. Document discharge plans carefully, taking into account all significant aspects of a client's hospitalization; reconcile apparently conflicting input and do not gloss over aspects of the chart.

6

Violence and Threats of Violence

A client's threat of suicide or homicide is among the most difficult situations a therapist will encounter (Jobes & O'Connor, 2008). There is a substantial body of professional literature regarding risk assessment of potentially violent behavior (Monahan & Steadman, 1994, 2001; Webster & Hucker, 2007). Authorities have emphasized the need for careful history taking, review of previous records, and compliance or lack of compliance with medication (Feldman, Moritz, & Benjamin, 2005; Simon, 2006a). In addition to the personal and professional challenges, such threats raise serious legal issues that we consider in this chapter. We first look at harm to self and then harm to others. Finally, we look at involuntary civil commitment, which has traditionally been a mechanism for intervening with dangerous clients to prevent harm, and premature release from institutions.

SUICIDE

Client suicides represent, according to the American Psychological Association (APA) Insurance Trust, approximately 4% of malpractice suits (Bennett et al., 2006). Bennett and his colleagues (2007) observed that the career-long odds of losing a client to suicide are one in five for psychologists and perhaps even higher for psychiatrists (Tsao & Layde, 2007). Indeed, the highest rate of claims filed against psychiatrists is for wrongful death due to suicide (Parry & Drogin, 2007).

It is difficult to be precise about figures because suicides are underreported (Parry & Drogin, 2007). Legal issues related to suicide probably occur more frequently in inpatient than in outpatient settings. Suicide is, of course, a complex phenomenon, and current research still does not allow for accurate predictions of suicide (Baerger & Bersoff, 2001).

The fact that a client or former client commits suicide does not mean that the therapist was negligent. "A mere error in professional judgment" associated with a suicide does not create liability (*Durney v. Terk*, 2007). There is no single, legally accepted standard of care for the treatment of suicidal clients. In most cases involving suicide, liability appears to focus on the foreseeability of the suicide and whether the actions of the practitioner were reasonable given that foreseeability. The problem, of course, is that foreseeability is something that has to be determined retrospectively. By and large, courts correctly focus on what the clinician knew or should have known at the time of the intervention (Jobes & O'Connor, 2008), but hindsight bias remains a problem in these cases.

Predicting the future accurately is not part of the standard of care; doing a careful assessment and developing a coherent treatment plan based on that assessment are (Berman, 2006). If a therapist carefully assesses the client for suicide, concludes that suicide is not reasonably foreseeable, and includes in the treatment plan periodic suicide assessments, the fact that the client commits suicide is not an adequate basis for liability (A. R. Smith et al., 2008).

The question arises, then, of what constitutes a comprehensive assessment of suicide potential (Tsao & Layde, 2007). There are myriad suicide assessment instruments, published by various psychological test companies. Some assessment of suicide is a routine part of a complete psychological evaluation of a client (Berman, 2006). Pope and Vasquez (2007), in fact, suggested that every intake evaluation include an assessment for suicidal ideation, regardless of whether such thinking is a part of the presenting problem of the client.

Whether the assessment is a structured interview; a series of scales on some general personality battery, such as the Minnesota Multiphasic Personality Inventory—2 (Tellegen et al., 2001) or the Personality Assessment Inventory (Morey, 2007); or a scale specifically designed to assess suicidal thinking is not important. As long as the instrument has been demonstrated to have construct validity in assessing the particular phenomenon, it will generally appear to have been a reasonable mechanism of assessing the suicide risk. For this same reason, it is important to not rely solely on a checklist that does not have such demonstrated validity. The importance of using one or more of these structured instruments is that doing so represents adherence to an established standard of care.

Pope and Vasquez (2007) constructed a very useful format for the assessment of suicide risk. They listed 21 factors that are based on the research and professional literature to conducted an informed suicide assessment:

- direct verbal warning,
- planning,
- past attempts,
- indirect statements and behavioral signs,
- depression,
- hopelessness,
- intoxication,
- presence of serious clinical syndromes in addition to the depression,
- sex,
- age,
- race,
- religion,
- living alone,
- bereavement,
- unemployment,
- physical illness,
- impulsivity,
- rigid thinking,
- stressful events,

- release from hospitalization, and
- a lack of a sense of belonging.

Pope and Vasquez stressed that all clients, not just those who are clinically depressed or having suicidal ideation, should be screened during the initial contact, and clinicians should remain sensitive to these issues during therapy.

One well-known suicide assessment scale is called the SAD PERSONS Scale (Patterson, Dohn, Bird, & Patterson, 1983), an acronym that highlights the major risk factors that research has demonstrated are often found in suicidal clients. The scale evaluates respondents on factors that can prompt feelings of Self-destruction, including gender (males are suicidal more often than females), Age, Depression, Prior history of suicide attempts, Ethanol abuse (alcohol as well as drug usage increases the risk), Rational thinking loss (any mental illness that interferes with logical thinking increases the risk), Support system loss (when family or friends are no longer around), an Organized plan, No significant other (again, a loss of support), and Sickness (of either the client or a loved one). Each factor is given a weight of 1, although clinical judgment in certain situations may make the weighting higher or lower.

In general, a score of 2 or less on the SAD PERSONS Scale is seen as representing minimal risk, and the respondent should have periodic checks. A score of 3 to 4 is seen as more serious, requiring more frequent observation. A score of 5 or 6 raises the possibility of hospitalization, and a score of 7 through 10 necessitates immediate hospitalization. In this approach, which is called *structured clinical judgment,* the dimensions to be explored are based on the available research, but within the exploration of those risk factors clinicians are free to follow their own clinical judgments.

Another approach that takes into account most of the relevant risk factors for suicide is a taxonomy designed by Rudd and Joiner (1998). They classified suicidality along a continuum from mild to extreme and based their assessments on observations of seven different areas. The first area, *predisposition,* includes such historical factors as previous suicidal ideation or attempts; abuse, or domestic violence; and such demographic factors as age, sex, marital status, and sociocultural background. The second area, called *precipitants*, generally refers to significant stressful events. The third area is *symptomatic presentation* and should include inquiries into such major psychiatric symptoms as depression, anxiety, obsessive–compulsive disorder, and substance abuse. The fourth area, which focuses on feelings of *hopelessness*, assesses the extent to which the individual feels that killing him- or herself is the "only way out." The fifth area is the *nature of the suicidal thinking* and refers to many of the qualitative inquiries with which clinicians are familiar when interviewing suicidal clients, such as the frequency of the thoughts and feelings, their intensity, their duration, how directed the intent appears to be, how specific the plans are, and whether the client has the means necessary to carry out the threat. The sixth area is *previous suicidal behavior* and considers, in addition to the previously noted historical factors, the frequency of attempts, the method of previous attempts, and whether they were done more as a "cry for help" than as genuine suicidal attempts; that is, were they performed such that someone else would most likely come to their rescue? If a person's prior suicide attempts were devoid of such third party involvement, it would clearly be a more ominous sign and signify a higher risk. The seventh area, *impulsivity*, can be assessed by interview, although a client trying to hide suicidal ideation may avoid discussing such matters.

In addition to asking questions about impulsivity, the clinician should have a complete medical and psychiatric history on the client or administer to the client some measure of impulsivity. One of the better known of these is the Barratt Impulsivity Scale (Barratt, 1965), a relatively brief questionnaire that evaluates dimensions of impulsivity without being transparent in what is being asked. The development and validation of this device were described by Monahan and Steadman (1994). The clinician should also make a careful inquiry into the client's substance abuse, of both illicit drugs and alcohol, because these can lead to decreased self-control and impairment of inhibitions. Finally, the therapist also should consider protective factors, such as social support and well-developed problem-solving skills, because these may prevent the acting out of suicidal ideation (Berman, Jobes, & Silverman, 2006).

Welch (2000) suggested using such risk factors to structure an initial, comprehensive suicide risk assessment and making follow-up assessments as an ongoing component of the treatment. He cautioned against the therapist denying the suicide risk, as well as not spending adequate time with the client to conduct a comprehensive assessment. He also suggested that if managed care questions the length of the assessment, the therapist point out that a lack of treatment could result in liability for both the therapist and the managed care company. He also suggested integrating family contact into the treatment plan and educating the client's family about signs of potential suicide. Finally, there should be adequate follow-up that is well documented in the client's record.

As noted in each of the risk assessment protocols just described, as well as in Monahan's (1981) work regarding prediction of violent behavior, suicide, like any kind of acting-out behavior, is best predicted by past behavior. A careful assessment should always include a careful history taking, with explorations of past direct and indirect suicidal behavior. Therapists who contend that the past is irrelevant and that they deal only with the here and now are taking a risky approach in dealing with the potential for self-destructive behavior.

Examples of bad practice that are likely negligent are failure to adequately examine the client; recognize the common risk factors associated with suicide; or appropriately provide treatment, restraint, or supervision. On the other hand, suicide does not equal malpractice, for several reasons (Berman et al., 2006). Courts understand that the threat of suicide needs to be balanced against other harms, including the risk of some medications or the unnecessary restraint of a client. As one court observed, "Calculated risks, of necessity, must be taken if the modern and enlightened treatment of the mentally ill is to be pursued intelligently and rationally. Neither the hospital nor the doctor are insurers of the client's health and safety" (*Baker v. United States*, 1964, p. 135). Practitioners are required only to take reasonable steps to prevent suicide.

Working against the therapist, however, is hindsight bias (Harley, 2007). The risk of suicide often appears more obvious after the fact than it did at the time that the treatment was being rendered.

Forming a coherent plan to deal with potential suicide is critical. A treatment plan, of course, must logically derive from the assessment. Within that plan the therapist may also be proactive in helping the client minimize environmental elements that can lead to increased risk, such as the presence of firearms or possession of quantities of medication that can lead to an overdose. The therapist should work with the client to find environmental supports, build on the client's strengths, explore suicidal fantasies, keep communications clear, be sensitive to his or her own negative feelings about the client, and communicate a caring attitude (Meyers, 1997).

Another issue in a comprehensive plan is coverage when the therapist is unavailable. The risk of suicide increases when the therapist is not present; therefore, good practice suggests the importance of careful planning regarding absences. These arrangements should be included in the treatment plan for any client for whom the potential for self-destructive behavior exists. The therapist should certainly inform subsequent health care providers of the client's suicidal tendencies (*Gross v. Allen*, 1994).

The question of "do-no-harm" contracts (signed statements by clients that they will not harm themselves or others) is sometimes raised as a potential defense to actions by or on behalf of a potentially suicidal or dangerous client (Garvey, Penn, Campbell, Esposito-Smythers, & Spirito, 2009). Whatever the therapeutic value, they provide little legal protection for the therapist should the client engage in self-destructive conduct. Such contracts may even look naive or like an admission that the therapist thought that the client was dangerous. In *Peck v. Addison County Counseling Service* (1985), for example, the court was critical of the counselor's obtaining a do-no-harm contract from the client who had been diagnosed with mental retardation.

Legal issues can also arise from the process of trying to prevent a potentially suicidal client from acting out. A particularly difficult issue is the degree to which family or others should be informed of a client's suicidal potential, so that they may be part of a protective plan. On one hand, this may energize the family to help prevent the suicide, but on the other hand it is a significant breach of confidentiality. In *Bellah v. Greenson* (1978), the therapist assessed his young adult client as suicidal, but he chose not to inform her parents. The client was addicted to drugs, and she eventually deliberately overdosed, and the parents sued the therapist for failure to tell them of their daughter's dangerousness. The court refused to extend a duty to inform the family in all cases of potential suicide.

Having a support network is seen as a protective factor in much of the risk assessment literature surrounding suicide. This provision of the treatment plan should be incorporated into the informed consent, making the dilemma of "disclose or not disclose" at a time of crisis less of a difficult decision (Cook, 2009). In other words, a competent client who has signed informed consent documentation has already consented to such disclosure, and this consent has been documented. It is unlikely that there is a risk of significant malpractice liability, however, when a therapist, after careful assessment and documentation, informs a family of the potential for a suicide (Welfel, 2008).

THE DUTY TO PROTECT (OR WARN)

The duty to protect as a legal cause of action derives from the case of *Tarasoff v. Regents of the University of California* (1976). This decision was a remarkable departure from the traditional legal rules. Mental health professionals traditionally have owed a duty of care to their clients but ordinarily did not owe duties to third parties (those whom a client might harm). *Tarasoff* changed that and has had a significant impact on the law (Monahan, 2008).

Prosenjit Poddar became obsessed with Tatiana Tarasoff, who he thought was spurning him. He saw psychologists at the University of California, Berkeley, mental health clinic. Clinic staff determined that Poddar might kill Tarasoff, and at one point staff called the campus police, who talked to Poddar and released him. Sometime later Poddar did kill Tarasoff, and her parents sued the clinic for failing to do enough to protect Tarasoff from a client whom clinic staff clearly saw as dangerous. (Poddar was tried for homicide, and when his conviction was overturned on appeal he was released on condition that he be deported to India; Blum, 1986.)

In the past, such suits were generally dismissed on the theory that there was no relationship between the clinic and the third party (Ms. Tarasoff) and hence the clinic owed her no legal duty (Behnke, Perlin, & Bernstein, 2005). The duty to warn had some precedent in other contexts, notably the duty of a public health official to warn the public of a communicable disease (*Hoffman v. Blackman,* 1970). Also, some courts had found a duty to protect third parties from clients in inpatient settings, at least when an institution could control the person. The duty of the therapist to the client arose from the therapist–client relationship, and no relationship existed with third parties to support a duty to them. *Tarasoff* essentially held that the duty to potential known victims arose from the practice of psychology itself (Cardi, 2009).

The case was initially phrased as a "duty to warn" (*Tarasoff v. Regents of the University of California,* 1974) and later cast more as a "duty to protect" (*Tarasoff v. Regents of the University of California,* 1976). The court noted that clinicians should still be able to exercise clinical discretion and that they do not need to become reporting automatons. The court noted that "proof aided by hindsight that the doctor judged wrongly was insufficient to establish negligence." The duty is still commonly called the *duty to warn,* but in fact warning is only one of several mechanisms that could be used to fulfill the duty to protect (Monahan, 2008). Other mechanisms may include, depending on the circumstances, increasing the frequency of sessions, changing medication, hospitalization, following through with child protective service (to protect a child), or contact law enforcement (Beck, 1990).

Several arguments have been advanced both for and against a *Tarasoff* duty. Those supporting such a duty to protect third parties argue that protecting life is more important than maintaining the confidences of psychotherapy. They also cite as precedent the lengthy history of the need for professionals to warn the public of public health hazards; dangerousness is merely seen as a different kind of public health hazard. Some have noted that for many years mental health professionals have predicted future dangerousness in court (e.g., in civil commitment and capital punishment cases), so there is no reason these professionals should not be able to identify dangerous clients (Meyers, 1997; S. R. Smith, 1996; Yufik, 2005).

The arguments against imposing such a duty on mental health professionals generally include the inability to accurately predict future violence; the interference with therapy that will occur as a result of the breach of confidentiality; and the fact that therapists tend to overpredict violence, leading to needless interruptions in therapy. In addition, opponents point out that warnings are usually ineffective in preventing violence and that potentially violent clients, fearing later consequences, will merely keep their violent thoughts to themselves. This creates a greater risk to the public because potentially violent individuals are not able to defuse their feelings by discussing them with a therapist. Thus, the costs to therapy are seen as exceeding the benefits of disclosure (Edwards, 2010b; Givelber, Bowers, & Blitch, 1984).

Tarasoff created a furor, some of it justified and much of it overblown. There was concern that there would be great liability for failing to accurately predict which clients would be dangerous. Despite a popular misconception, liability in the *Tarasoff* case did not lie in the failure to predict the violent behavior. The psychologist had accurately predicted that Poddar was dangerous. In fact, Givelber and colleagues (1984) found that none of the liability in the duty-to-protect cases that they reviewed centered on the lack of predictive ability. Instead, frequently cited causes for the findings of liability were failure to follow standard procedures in assessment; failure to consult with colleagues; and failure to document the assessment, the consultations, and how the assessments led to a particular kind of intervention or management strategy (Monahan, 2006).

After *Tarasoff* there was also great concern that warning (and, therefore, breaches of confidentiality) would occur any time a client made a threat. In fact, courts have made it clear that it is not a threat or a vague possibility of harming others that establishes a duty to protect, but a believable threat of actual harm. However, psychologists continue to misunderstand their state laws, with more than 75% of them assuming that warning is the only option (Pabian, Welfel, & Beebe, 2009).

The emphasis on duty to warn has been misplaced (Walcott, Cerundolo, & Beck, 2001). Subsequent commentators (e.g., Beck 1990) have suggested a wide range of possible interventions when the client makes threats toward third parties, depending on the outcome of the therapist's assessment of the client. These may include increasing the number of therapy sessions; referring the client for a medication consultation; changing the client's medication; giving the client one's home phone, cell phone, and/or pager number; having the client voluntarily admit him- or herself to a hospital; filing involuntary commitment papers; bringing the intended victim into the treatment session; and, as a last resort, notifying the authorities and/or the intended victim (Monahan, 2008).

Although most states have created some form of a *Tarasoff*-like liability, courts have tended to make the liability fairly narrow. That approach is illustrated by a fairly famous incident in which James Brady was injured when John Hinckley tried to kill President Ronald Reagan (*Brady v. Hopper*, 1984). The suit alleged that Dr. John Hopper, Hinckley's psychiatrist, knew or "should have known" of his client's violent tendencies. Brady did not succeed in the litigation. It became apparent, as the evidence unfolded, that Hinckley had not discussed his violent fantasies with Hopper. The court noted that even if Hopper had known of Hinckley's infatuation with Jodie Foster, his preoccupation with the movie *Taxi Driver*, and his target practice at pictures of Ronald Reagan, all of this taken together would not constitute a foreseeable risk. This is important because it narrows the guesswork involved and the tendency to indulge in hindsight bias (Harley, 2007). The clinician does not have to make predictions beyond what the state of the art allows regarding such predictions (A. R. Smith et al., 2008).

Ordinarily, a clear, and usually direct, threat of physical violence is necessary for liability. In addition, many states require that the threat be directed toward an identifiable victim. A believable threat against a large group, the public, or an organization is usually not enough to create *Tarasoff* liability. In such a case, even if the therapist has been negligent there is no legal duty (and therefore no liability) to the injured third parties. Werth, Welfel, and Benjamin (2008) provided a series of perspectives on the duty to warn.

Among the issues that remain unsettled is whether the therapist must receive threats directly from the client or whether information passed to the therapist from another source is sufficient to trigger the *Tarasoff* obligations. For several years after the *Tarasoff* case, the trend seemed to be toward requiring that the information come directly from the client (Yufik, 2005). A case in California, however, extended the duty when the client's threat of violence was communicated to the therapist by a family member. In *Ewing v. Goldstein* (2004), the therapist was treating a client who was distraught over his breakup with his girlfriend. When the therapist subsequently spoke to the client's father, the father told the therapist about threats his son had made against his ex-girlfriend's new boyfriend. The therapist arranged to have the son hospitalized, but the admitting psychiatrist did not see him as suicidal and insisted on discharging him the next day. The day after that, the son murdered the new boyfriend and committed suicide. The parents of the boyfriend then sued the therapist. The appellate court stated that a communication made by a family member for the purpose of advancing the client's treatment is a "patient communication" and therefore triggers the duty to protect. The extent to which this approach will be adopted in future cases generally remains to be seen.

So-called *Tarasoff* statutes have been adopted in a number of states (Hales, Yudofsky, & Gabbard, 2008). There are several different models, but usually they require a direct communication to the therapist of a believable threat against an identifiable intended victim (Benjamin, Kent, & Sirikantraporn, 2008). There are efforts in some states to carve out "safe harbors" for therapists, so that if they have notified authorities or developed a comprehensive treatment plan to deal with threats, liability may be limited (Edwards, 2010a). Many of these statutes are not very well written (Huffman, 2008). Even when there has been an effort to limit liability, faulty drafting of the necessary documents may not achieve this purpose (Kachigian & Felthous, 2004; S. R. Smith, 1986–1987).

A *Tarasoff* statute may also not be successful in reducing *Tarasoff* liability if the statute does not specifically indicate that it is abrogating other common law liability. Courts may find that the statute supplements, not replaces, common law liability (e.g., *Dawe v. Bar-Levav,* 2010).

To avoid expanding the breach of confidentiality associated with warning potential victims, or the authorities, some legal professionals (e.g., Klinka, 2009) have suggested that the warnings not be seen as waiving the therapist–client privilege, which disclosures to third parties usually destroy. Ordinarily, disclosure of information regarding therapy destroys the privilege covering that information (see Chapter 8, this volume). This is not a settled question, but there is some legal support for maintaining the privilege even in the face of a warning to intended victims (*United States v. Hayes,* 2000; Benjamin et al., 2008).

The duty to protect is a negligence action. In essence, a negligence action regarding a failed duty to protect alleges that a practitioner did not act in a reasonable way in protecting an identifiable third party and therefore breached the standard of care expected of therapists. The unusual part of this duty is that it is to third parties, not to clients, but the focus nevertheless is primarily what the therapist did in assessing and managing the client's treatment. As such, these cases demand careful assessment; well-documented consultation; and a plan of treatment, intervention, or management that logically and directly flows from the assessment (Werth et al., 2008). In *Higgins v. Salt Lake County* (1993), the mother of a girl stabbed by a client who had been seen by (among others) county mental health professionals sued those professionals and the county. The court said that liability could be based on the failure of the professionals to conduct a proper examination and diagnosis if that examination would have revealed the potential violence and also an intended and identifiable victim of the violence. (Sovereign immunity precluded liability in this case, however.)

As in other negligence cases, when addressing duty-to-protect issues courts defer to clinical judgment that is reasonable and based on a comprehensive assessment. In *White v. United States* (1986), a client who had grounds privileges at a psychiatric hospital was regularly leaving the grounds to visit his wife, who lived nearby. This was a technical violation of grounds privileges, although the client always returned to the hospital on time. The client told his therapist about violent fantasies he had been having toward his wife. The therapist carefully evaluated the client's fantasies; consulted with colleagues; requested updated psychological testing; and concluded, on the basis of this comprehensive assessment, that these were merely fantasies rather than actual intentions to do bodily harm. The therapist was wrong, and the client stabbed his wife multiple times with a pair of scissors. The court determined that although the hospital was negligent for allowing the client to leave the grounds, the therapist was not negligent because she gave a compelling description of how she met the standard of care in doing her assessment and selecting a course of treatment that she believed was appropriate.

A question that arises in the duty to protect deals with clients with HIV/AIDS. Simone and Fulero (2001) presented research that indicates that mental health professionals are in essence split down the middle regarding whether third parties should be notified in such circumstances: Neither the diagnosis nor the mode of viral transmission significantly influence clinicians' decisions to breach confidentiality. Others have observed that some states have taken the position that they will not extend the doctrine of duty to protect third parties in HIV and AIDS cases unless there is an imminent threat of physical violence. The cases have not been consistent from state to state (*Doe v. High Tech Institute*, 1998; *Garcia v. Santa Rosa Health Care Corporation*, 1996; *Lemon v. Stewart*, 1996; *N.O.L. v. District of Columbia*, 1995). Similar issues related to warning family members about known genetic defects could arise in the future (Welfel, 2008).

It is possible that liability could arise for breach of confidentiality when a mental health professional warns a possible victim but the possibility of violence is remote. Some states specifically authorize such disclosures by statute (Confidentiality of Alcohol and Drug Abuse Patient Records, 2010), and it is generally implied in states with *Tarasoff* statutes. In most of these states, it seems likely that something more than negligence would be needed to support a claim based on breach of confidentiality. As long as the breach of confidentiality is made in good faith with reasonable examination and diagnosis, and without unnecessary public disclosure, liability is unlikely for negligence, breach of contract, or breach of privacy (Huffman, 2008).

The costs and benefits of *Tarasoff* continue to be debated. Some evidence suggests that the duty to warn harms rather than protects the public in that therapists, fearful of litigation, will decline to provide treatment to clients with a history of violent behavior, leaving them more likely to commit acts of violence in the future (Edwards, 2010b). Additional empirical work is important to determine the effect of the *Tarasoff* duty.

CIVIL COMMITMENT AND LIABILITY

Civil commitment—incarcerating someone for what the person is predicted to do, not for criminal misconduct—is a very powerful legal concept. As a result of the extraordinary power of civil commitment, the courts have constructed a number of constitutional, procedural, and substantive protections to avoid abuse. The U.S. Supreme Court, for example, has held that the Constitution requires that states prove the criteria for commitment by "clear and convincing evidence" because of the serious infringement of a committed individual's liberty and to reduce the chance that a harmless individual might be erroneously confined (*Addington v. Texas*, 1979).

The following is a brief summary of the state laws regarding commitment. Mental health professionals who are going to be involved with the civil commitment process should study the commitment process in greater detail, understand commitment law in their states, and consult with colleagues who have experience in commitment. In most states commitment is based on a determination that someone is mentally ill and as a result of the mental illness is imminently dangerous to self or others, or cannot provide for the necessities of life (gravely disabled; Bloom, 2004; Simon, 2006b). Adolescents pose special issues because it is sometimes difficult to determine whether their parents may voluntarily admit them or they are subject to civil commitment (Borum, 2009; A. L. Miller & Emanuele, 2009).

In most states, mental health professionals, police, and others are authorized to present a person to a designated mental health facility (Ferris, 2008). If mental health professionals at the facility find that the person probably is mentally ill and dangerous, the person may be held at the facility for a short time, pending a more complete evaluation and judicial hearing (Ferris, 2008). After a hearing a judge may order the commitment of the person to the facility. The person is released when the mental health professionals no longer believe that the person meets the requirements for commitment or when an additional judicial hearing makes that determination. In recent years *outpatient commitment,* in which a person who meets the basic standards for commitment but may live in the community provided that person is subject to supervision (e.g., in regard to taking medications), has become common (Allbright, Levy, & Wagle, 2002; Sherer; 2007).

An informal, but important, element of the civil commitment process is the leverage that the threat of commitment gives therapists to get a client to agree to a voluntary admission (Bloom, 2004). The voluntary approach is easier, more flexible, and probably carries less stigma than commitment, but it does not have the due process protection of a formal commitment. Voluntary commitment requires, however, that the client be competent to make the decision to be hospitalized (*Zinermon v. Burch,* 1990).

A form of civil commitment that is currently receiving considerable attention is that of sex predator or violent sex offender laws (Hung & Chamberlain, 2009). These laws, which are more like sexual psychopath laws (which in the 1950s and 1960s allowed the confinement of those with the "propensity to commit sexual offenses") than traditional civil commitment, confine sex offenders to a mental institution following the end of a prison term, until they are deemed no longer dangerous (Deming, 2008; Drogin, 2008).

Civil commitment's mix of power and regulation would seem to be ripe for malpractice suits, yet there have not been many successful malpractice cases against psychologists for wrongful involuntary commitment. This is the case for several reasons, one of which is that states usually provide a defense for mental health professionals who participate in committing someone if the professional has acted in good faith. An example of acting in bad faith would be a case in which a doctor, for purely personal animus, certifies a commitment or falsifies an affidavit (Binder, 2002).

The degree to which courts have extended latitude to mental health professionals in the commitment process is illustrated by *Tracz v. Charter Centennial Peaks* (2000). The plaintiff, Ms. Tracz, attended a free mental health screening where she apparently expressed both suicidal and homicidal ideation. The psychiatrist and counselor the center that sponsored the screening then authorized a 72-hr hold, and she was transported to the facility, where she attempted to walk out but was restrained. Within an hour after being taken to a second facility, she was evaluated and released upon promising that she would seek outpatient treatment. She then filed a civil suit alleging claims for false imprisonment, outrageous conduct, professional negligence, and assault and battery. One issue Tracz raised was that the psychiatrist who signed the hold-and-treat order had not personally examined her but had relied on the observations of the mental health counselor who had examined her. The court held that the statute did not require an in-person evaluation but allowed the hold to be authorized on the basis of the observations of someone whom the psychiatrist reasonably believed to be reliable. Ethically, however, psychologists are not supposed to make statements regarding, diagnoses of, or conclusions about someone they have not examined unless they clarify the reasons why such an in-person evaluation was not done and qualify their conclusions in terms of the limited validity and reliability of using third party information. Rural areas without in-person access to mental health professionals present special problems for conducting civil commitment assessments.

Liability for participating in civil commitment confinement (after the initial temporary hold) is also limited by the fact that most civil commitments are determined by a judge, with mental health professionals simply testifying as experts giving their opinions. Most states provide significant immunity to witnesses (Binder, 2002). In addition, civil commitments are based on predictions of whether someone is dangerous, and such predictions are more a matter of opinion than scientific precision (Slogobin, 2006).

This is not to say that there is never liability for the commitment process. A classic case is *Whitree v. State* (1968). Whitree was a client confined in the New York state hospital system for 14 years. His suit alleged negligence and false imprisonment, among other things. In finding for Whitree, the court observed that he had been examined very rarely, and then only superficially. The court also found the psychiatric records inadequate and that the primary reason for the length of the hospitalization was the inadequate psychiatric care.

A state that violates clear constitutional requirements, or other federal law, risks facing liability through civil rights or disability rules. The U.S. Supreme Court has imposed procedural limits on commitment, which we have discussed in this chapter (e.g., clear and convincing evidence that a person intends to harm self or others, voluntarily committed clients must be competent). The Court has been more reluctant to create substantial rights to treatment for involuntary clients. It has, however, created limited rights to treatment.

In *O'Connor v. Donaldson* (1975), the U.S. Supreme Court held that it is unconstitutional to confine without treatment a nondangerous individual who is capable of surviving outside of the hospital. The Court did not address whether the state may confine a dangerous person without treatment or whether it could confine a nondangerous client if it does provide treatment. Mr. Donaldson had been confined in a hospital in Florida for 30 years with very little treatment and no proof that he was violent. Donaldson claimed that although he was not violent, he had been confined involuntarily without treatment.

The Court has also held that under the Americans With Disabilities Act of 1990, states are, where possible, required to provide persons with mental health conditions community-based treatment instead of placement in institutions (*Olmstead v. L. C.,* 1999). The conditions of confinement have at times resulted in lawsuits; involuntary clients have the right to reasonable safety and minimally adequate care (*Youngberg v. Romeo,* 1982). These federal cases are primarily directed at state or institutional liability, not the liability of individual professionals.

The reluctance of courts to impose professional liability in the commitment process is not an excuse for sloppy practice, of course. Persons who are involuntarily incarcerated, even though this is a civil rather than a criminal process, deserve the most careful consideration. The approach should comprise the usual good practice, consistent with ethical standards, of a careful history, diagnosis, solid treatment plan, and frequent reviews of progress, regardless of whether these are enforced by the courts.

PREMATURE RELEASE

Suppose a client is released from involuntary commitment without a careful assessment of his condition or despite a notation in his chart that he is making threats against his family. That afternoon he kills his sister and commits suicide. Does the mental health institution face liability for the decision to release him? Sadly, a number of actual cases raise this issue. The release of an involuntary client may be pursuant to a court order or directive, in which case there is little likelihood of liability if the staff have provided the court with solid information. In most states, release is more likely to occur on the decision of the hospital staff that the conditions that justified commitment are no longer present.

The potential legal consequences of the clearly erroneous release of a dangerous client can be significant. The possibility of a violent result is not trivial, and when the bad event happens, it is serious. Property damage, personal injury, homicide, and suicide are all possible. These are among the most serious injuries and can result in substantial damages. In this section, we distinguish between the release of involuntary and voluntary clients. Not all states agree, but there has been a trend toward imposing liability for the negligent, premature release of involuntary clients (*Hamman v. County of Maricopa,* 1989; *Naidu v. Laird,* 1988; *Perreira v. State,* 1989). It is ordinarily permissible to persuade a released client to continue treatment on a voluntary basis.

The courts find that this duty to third parties arises out of the fact that the mental health institution staff have virtually complete control over the client and should be in a good position to know whether the client is dangerous (Martin, 2007). However, this is not absolute liability. Indeed, courts have given considerable deference to the clinical judgments of professionals who release clients, so long as the decision is made on the basis of a careful diagnosis, with good information available on which to make release decisions. Mechanisms for careful evaluation prior to release have been in place in many institutions for some time (Travin & Bluestone, 1987).

Courts commonly use the phrases *reasonable professional care* or *professional judgment* in cases of premature release ("Scope of Psychiatrist's Liability," 1990). One reason for this deference to therapists' decisions to release involuntary clients may be the understanding that holding involuntary clients longer than necessary is a serious infringement on the personal liberty of an innocent person. That must be balanced against the risks associated with the person being free (Till, 1993).

The premature release of voluntary inpatients may arise in several forms. One is a client who leaves the institution against medical advice. In that circumstance, if the therapist believes that the person will be dangerous outside the institution, there are limited options. One is to persuade the person to stay and, barring that, ensure that the client leaves the institution with as much follow-up care as possible. Another is to consider starting involuntary-commitment proceedings to prevent the person's release. The other option is to notify the authorities, or the possible victims (if they are identifiable), under a *Tarasoff* approach. In any event, particularly careful documentation of what happened and why is essential.

More problematic legally is a situation in which the therapists or institution staff dismiss a client from the institution inappropriately. This may occur because of inadequate diagnosis and care, failure to maintain good communications among caregivers, inadequate record keeping, or the client's inability to pay hospital fees.

Courts recognize that institutions have less control over voluntary than involuntary clients. The decisions have not uniformly found liability for premature release of voluntary clients and, where it has been found, it is often based on especially bad practice. An example of this negligence is *DeJesus v. United States Department of Veteran Affairs* (2007). The client was an inpatient in a Veterans Affairs hospital, diagnosed with serious mental problems, and had behaved violently, but was released by the facility. Shortly thereafter he shot and killed four children and then himself. Liability was based on the facts that no employee at the hospital knew his complete medical history because the record keeping was so bad, the hospital failed to come to a clear conclusion about this mental illness, and it did not try to prevent his release despite his violent tendencies (Martin, 2007). The court found that such sloppiness amounted to gross negligence.

Another reason for the premature release of a client is pressure from managed care (*Wilson v. Blue Cross*, 1990). These situations become especially difficult when the clinical judgment of the staff is that the client is in need of more treatment but the time period authorized by the insurance company for the hospital stay has expired. The hospital may appeal to the insurance company for more time, but what happens when the insurance carrier denies that request? Although liability will depend on the specific circumstances and the nature of the hospitalization, in the usual case of a private client who is hospitalized there is a clear duty to the client, regardless of the reimbursement arrangements. It is, for example, no defense for the negligent release of a client that private insurance or Medicare will no longer cover the cost of the hospital care. Referral to another provider, if done properly and voluntarily, with continuity of care, may be legally permissible (Appelbaum, 1996).

The clinicians responsible for the release of a client who may represent a potential danger to self or others are expected to exercise reasonable care in their decision making. When they decide to discharge the client, there needs to be a careful consideration of the presenting problem at the time of admission and documentation of how the problem was handled or resolved during the client's stay at the hospital. If the reason for admission had to do with violent behavior, the record must reflect how the factors leading to that violence were addressed during the treatment. Vague phrases such as "Client has achieved maximum hospital benefits" will not be adequate in such situations. For example, if a client was admitted because of violent behavior caused by her or his response to command hallucinations, the record must make clear how the illness that created the command hallucinations has been treated. If the violent behavior came from the client's failure to comply with taking prescribed medication, the treatment plan and progress notes must reflect how the issue of noncompliance has been dealt with (e.g., evidence that the client is motivated to take medication, or that the medication will now be given in an injectable form).

In short, "economic discharge" of a client from a hospital carries risk to a hospital and to the professionals involved. When the client is still potentially violent, the institution and the professional take substantial risks when releasing that person (Calfee, 1998).

PRACTICAL SUGGESTIONS

1. It is good practice for every intake evaluation to include an assessment for suicidal or other violent ideation, regardless of whether such thinking is a part of the presenting problem.
2. Forming a coherent plan to deal with potential suicide is critical. A treatment plan, of course, must logically derive from the assessment. The plan should include arrangements for those times the therapist is absent.
3. The *Tarasoff* cases created a new legal duty to the identifiable victims of clients. This liability usually occurs when the therapist understands the client was or could be dangerous but fails to take reasonable steps to protect known victims. Warning potential victims is one, but not the only, way of protecting them.
4. The duty to protect is a negligence action. The claim is that the practitioner did not act in a reasonable way and therefore breached the standard of care expected of therapists. The best defense comprises careful assessment; well-documented consultation; and a plan of treatment, intervention, or management that logically and directly flows from the assessment.
5. Mental health professionals who are involved with the civil commitment process should understand the commitment law in their state and consult with colleagues who have experience in commitment.

6. Although there are many legal protections for therapists who partic-
    ipate in the commitment process, it is essential that they act in good
    faith, which includes acting honestly and for legally appropriate
    motives.

7. The reluctance of courts to impose professional liability in the com-
    mitment process is not an excuse for sloppy practice. The approach
    should be the usual good practice of a careful history and diagnosis,
    solid treatment plans, and frequent reviews of progress.

8. Premature release of involuntary clients creates greater potential
    legal liability than hospitalization itself. Courts, however, usually
    defer to the clinical judgments of professionals.

9. If you believe that a voluntary client who leaves the institution
    against medical advice will be dangerous outside the institution, con-
    sider the options: persuading the person to stay, providing as much
    care as possible outside the institution, starting involuntary commit-
    ment proceedings, notifying the authorities, or notifying (if they are
    identifiable) any intended victims. In any event, know that particu-
    larly careful documentation of what happened and why is essential.

10. Avoid the premature release of voluntary clients that can come from
    inadequate diagnosis or care, failure to maintain good communica-
    tions among caregivers, or inadequate record keeping. Economic
    release of clients who may be dangerous is legally very risky for both
    the institution and the professional.

7

Other Areas of Liability in Practice

Almost any area of practice can result in malpractice claims. Some areas raise special problems (Austin, Moline, & Williams, 1990). In this chapter, we review specific areas of practice (e.g., working with children, forensics), areas of misconduct (e.g., sex with clients, defamation) and special activities (e.g., research, prescribing pharmaceuticals). All are areas in which special care is warranted; in short: *Caveat professio.*

SEXUAL MISCONDUCT

This could be the shortest section of the book: Sexual contact with clients is malpractice. It is unethical, and every psychologist knows this, and it creates clear liability. We will, however, add a few details.

Disturbing statistics regarding sexual involvement with clients were published as early as 1977: Six percent of male psychologist respondents and 0.6% of female psychologist respondents admitted to having had sexual relations with a client, and 80% of those admitted to having done so repeatedly (Holroyd & Brodsky, 1977). Of course, the real number is probably somewhat higher because there may well be many psychologists who do not admit to this behavior (Pope, 1994).

Sexual misconduct remains a major cause of successful malpractice actions, although according to the American Psychological Association (APA) Insurance Trust, it is not as frequent as it has been. The reasons for the decrease are not clear, although Bennett et al. (2006) suggested that at least one reason is that state licensing boards have become more aggressive in pursuing disciplinary actions against psychologists who are involved in sexual misconduct. In addition, several states have criminalized such behavior (Strasburger, Jorgenson, & Randles, 2008). Other possible explanations for the phenomenon are that there are more female therapists and that the number of female therapists involved in sexual misconduct is much lower than the number of male therapists. Finally, the fact that sexual misconduct has come out of the closet, so to speak, and is being discussed more openly and frankly in graduate training programs may also account for some of the decrease (Ebert, 2006).

Courts find liability when a therapist is in a sexual relationship with a current client; expert testimony is generally not required to determine that this is a deviation from the standard of care. However, decisions regarding injury and the extent of damages may still require expert testimony to guide the court (Pope, 1994).

There generally must be a professional relationship between the therapist and the client for a sexual relationship to result in malpractice. The questions raised in Chapter 3 about when a professional relationship exists can be important in some cases. Sex with an acquaintance may not give rise to liability, although sex with the same person, if a client, would.

The question of how long the professional relationship lasts can be important. Prior to 1992, the APA (2010) "Ethical Principles of Psychologists and Code of Conduct" prohibited sexual contact with clients. It said nothing explicitly about former clients, but licensing boards generally interpreted this to mean no sex with former clients, a position they could not always maintain in court (*Elliott v. North Carolina Psychology Board*, 1998). The current APA Ethics Code prohibits sexual relationships with a former client for 2 years following termination of treatment and, after

2 years, only under "the most unusual circumstances." In essence, the therapist has to bear the burden of proving seven factors, including that there was no exploitation of the client, no evidence of a termination of therapy in order to pursue a sexual relationship, and no evidence of using knowledge gained in therapy to manipulate the client. If a former client were to file a complaint, however, it would be difficult for the therapist to prove that there was no exploitation.

Some other codes of conduct, notably that of the Association of State and Provincial Psychology Boards (2005), state that because clients are generally part of a vulnerable population, who have put trust in the therapist, it is difficult for a therapist to establish that a posttermination sexual involvement did not involve some degree of exploitation. Some states, in fact, have interpreted this as a perpetuity rule, meaning that it is a violation of professional standards ever to become involved with a client or former client. Sexual misconduct by psychologists is covered by the Florida Statute of Sexual Misconduct (1991 & Supp. 1998; repealed for review). The Florida administrative code Sexual Misconduct in the Practice of Psychology (2010) no longer states an absolute perpetuity rule but lists factors to be considered. Perpetuity rules are disfavored by courts and may well run afoul of state constitutional provisions (*Caddy v. Florida Department of Health,* 2000).

In addition to prohibiting sexual relationships with clients, ethical standards also prohibit sexual relations between the therapist and the clients' close relatives or significant others and from accepting as clients persons with whom they have engaged in sexual intimacies (APA, 2010). If the client is injured as a result of the therapist's sexual contact with someone else, the therapist could be liable. An interesting question is whether there is also a duty to the relative if the relative is harmed. When carried to extremes (in perpetuity), these limitations on personal relationships between therapists and clients and others may be a violation of constitutional rights of privacy and association (*Caddy v. Florida Department of Health,* 2000; Gorman, 2009).

A few therapists have talked and written about the therapeutic value of sexual relations (S. R. Smith, 1991, p. 227). Although the majority of mental health professionals reject this position, as do all professional associations, what would happen if such a therapist were to try to justify his or her behavior on the basis of this "school of thought"? It is unlikely that this position would be viewed as being endorsed by a respectable minority with sufficient professional or scientific grounding to justify it as a legitimate school of thought. Some therapists have tried to argue that sexual contact is acceptable because of what they call a "true love exception" (claiming the prohibition on sexual relations is overcome if the client and therapist are genuinely in love or get married). This exception is a myth. Despite this, surveys of therapists reveal a remarkable lack of knowledge of these matters. Although the figures are probably somewhat lower now, a survey of 1,300 therapists in 1987 revealed that almost 30% of the sample believed that posttermination sexual contact could be appropriate, and about 17% believed that the APA Ethics Code allowed it (S. R. Smith, 1991).

In a malpractice case, inappropriate sexual relations with a client demonstrates a breach of duty, but a successful plaintiff must still prove causation and injury/damages, no matter how outrageous the malpractice. In *Carmichael v. Carmichael* (1991), the therapist, during the course of treatment, convinced the client to have sex with him, leave her marriage, and marry him. When they later divorced, she claimed that his actions, as a therapist, were exploitative and caused her serious emotional harm. The court could not find a causal link between her claims of emotional distress and the improper sexual relationship.

Sexual misconduct may give rise to several torts. Battery is a possibility, under the theory that the client cannot give legal consent to sexual touching while in therapy. Intentional infliction of emotional distress is possible because the sexual conduct has such a high possibility of causing harm. Negligence also is a possibility. In addition, such conduct may be a crime (Illingworth, 1995).

A number of liability policies of insurance companies refuse to provide coverage for intentional torts or for sexual misconduct. Plaintiffs and therapist–defendants, therefore, have incentives to find a way to make negligence the basis for claims against the therapist for sexual misconduct. Mishandling the transference phenomenon has been one approach, as illustrated by *Zipkin v. Freeman* (1968). In that case, Dr. Freeman persuaded a client to go on overnight trips with him and took the client to nude swimming parties that were called "group therapy." Freeman told his client that her symptoms would return if she did not continue her treatment, and she eventually left her husband and moved into an apartment in the same building as Freeman's office. Freeman was found liable for the client's injuries based on his mishandling of her transference, and the insurance company was obligated to pay this because the case arose out of a failure to render proper treatment.

Although basing these cases on negligent mishandling of transference is a matter of some debate, it is a common approach in malpractice cases. One federal court noted that "when the therapist mishandles transference and becomes sexually involved with a patient, medical authorities are nearly unanimous in considering such conduct to be malpractice" (*Simmons v. United States*, 1986, p. 1365).

Cases of sexual misconduct are often instances of "he said, she said" without other clear evidence. As a result, the therapist can face the very difficult circumstance in which charges of sexual misconduct are fraudulent or brought by clients who are acting out some primitive retaliation fantasies against the therapist. The frequency of such complaints is, of course, unknown. The therapist is left trying to prove that nothing happened. This becomes especially problematic because conscientious and caring therapists are reluctant to use their own client's psychopathology as a way of defending themselves.

Hedges (2007) provided sound advice for therapists falsely accused of sexual misconduct. He recommended that when clients state a sexual interest in the therapist, "be sure to document what they said, how you responded, your consultation with a peer, and how you systematically followed it up" (p. 47). If the client then "tells you a dream in which you are a sexualized or idealized participant, in either a clear or disguised way, document and consult" (p. 47). Hedges was basically telling therapists that they must document the very topics that they find most disturbing and would like to sweep under the rug. Most therapists have not received formal, systematic education in how to deal with such situations.

Hedges (2007) went on to highlight certain "danger signals that therapists need to be aware of and prepared to deal with, such as the client showing excessive interest in the therapist's personal life" (p. 48). He also offered very concrete suggestions for how to deal with the countertransference that therapists may experience in such situations:

> When a client appears in your fantasies or dreams, document it outside of the record first, then consult with a colleague, and consider including it in the record. Seek consultation whenever you find you are reluctant to consider a client in clinical terms or find yourself interpreting client material in terms of symbols or experiences that come from your own life. (p. 48)

The advice is basically that one treat a highly eroticized reaction of a client to a therapist, or vice versa, as one would any other manifestation of psychopathology: Consult and document.

NONTRADITIONAL THERAPIES

A classic case of nontraditional therapy involved a very charismatic psychiatrist/psychoanalyst, Dr. John Rosen. Rosen had developed a treatment technique for clients with schizophrenia that he called *direct analysis,* and he wrote a book by the same name (Rosen, 1953). Rosen believed that individuals with schizophrenia had regressed to a very primitive stage of psychological development and that a therapist could assist the client by speaking directly to the unconscious, making interpretations of primitive symbolic material. In this case, Rosen was treating a client, Alice Hammer, in his private psychiatric hospital, and during the course of one of the sessions Rosen allegedly assaulted Hammer. Hammer then sued Rosen (*Hammer v. Rosen,* 1960) and Rosen, in his defense, tried to argue that his new form of psychotherapy permitted such physical assault. Rosen testified that the technique required communication on the client's level and could include slapping and hitting as a means to facilitate this communication. The judge disagreed and found Rosen liable for damages to Hammer.

In *Abraham v. Zaslow* (1975; Alexander & Scheflin, 1998), Dr. Zaslow, a psychologist, practiced "rage reduction techniques" with his clients, which involved extensive physical stimulation of the client's rib cage. Abraham, the client, claimed physical injuries as a result of the treatment, and the jury awarded him $170,000 in damages.

Innovative or nontraditional therapies require special caution (S. R. Smith & Meyer, 1987). Traditional therapies carry known risks and benefits, which may be less clear for innovative therapies. For that reason, full disclosure and enhanced informed consent become especially important (Gans, 1999). The therapist should be sure to obtain a detailed and competent informed consent to the treatment, making certain the client is aware that the treatment is novel or experimental and knows all the risks and benefits of the treatment approach. It is important that clients are also mentally competent to make such a choice and have made that treatment decision voluntarily.

Treatment programs growing out of the sensitivity training methods of the 1960s have led to some allegations of injuries. In one such instance, in which group participants were naked and in hot tubs, a man suffered a heart attack and died (Cohen, 1979). His family sued the treatment center. The idea behind this form of treatment was, according to Cohen (1979), based on a theory that nudity would facilitate self-disclosure and acceptance of one's physical attributes. There has been a recent resurgence of interest in a technique called *primal scream,* which also was very popular in the 1960s. Participants in primal scream groups are encouraged to regress, and some wind up writhing on the floor; some injuries have ensued, and some group participants have filed suit for damages sustained (Cohen, 1979).

These nontraditional, or pop, therapies can create liability issues in several ways. If practitioners make guarantees or similar claims that cannot be met, they may face breach-of-contract claims (Epstein, 1976). If they knowingly misrepresent the efficacy of treatment, consumer fraud claims are possible. In terms of malpractice, they may create liability by directly mistreating a participant (e.g., having the client participate in a sweat lodge that can cause heat prostration and death). In at least two cases, practitioners of the Lifespring Movement (new age/human potential training, in which authoritarian trainers enforce various rules) were sued because of psychological injuries sustained by participants. Both cases were settled (*Bingham v. Lifespring,* 1985; *Suskind v. Lifespring,* 1984).

Nontraditional/pop therapies may also create liability by attracting someone away from a treatment that would have been effective. They may lack any careful screening procedure that would identify clients who are too emotionally ill to benefit from the particular treatment or who may in fact be harmed by it. For example, the encounter group movement, popular in the 1970s, encouraged sharing of intense emotional experiences in a group setting. There were few established standards for "leaders" or no leaders at all for these encounter groups, or sensitivity training groups. The movement spawned a number of lawsuits due to the psychological harm resulting from the aggressive and emotional confrontations.

Bennett et al. (2006) argued that practitioners embarking on a new or innovative treatment need to evaluate the evidence, spell out a rationale for why certain techniques are appropriate for certain clients, and note why this particular client is an appropriate candidate for the new treatment approach. Therapy approaches that are gaining acceptance and use, but that are still new or nontraditional, require special attention. E-therapy, in which mental health services are delivered online, is a current example. Special concerns regarding informed consent and referral, for example, arise from such nontraditional therapies (Recupero & Rainey, 2005).

RESEARCH

Psychological research has not given rise to substantial malpractice liability. There is, however, the potential for liability when one is conducting psychological studies. Two examples illustrate potential liability, one of which resulted in a suit (the other did not). In the first example, a group of researchers working on experimental mind control techniques gave some subjects LSD without their knowledge or consent. This resulted in a suicide and a lawsuit (*Thornwell v. United States,* 1979). In the second example, a much different circumstance, the famous Milgram (1974) study, subjects were told to deliver strong, up to lethal-level, shocks to other subjects (who were actually confederates only pretending to receive the shocks). The subjects were intentionally placed in a very stressful situation. Several torts were implicated in these two experiments, notably battery in the LSD case and intentional infliction of emotional distress in the Milgram research (Gordon, 1969).

The tort liability principles discussed throughout the book apply to both experimental and clinical research (Gordon, 1969). In addition, the potential for serious abuse of human subjects in research is so great that, beginning with the Nuremberg trials of Nazis, a series of legal protections of subjects have been established (University of Minnesota, 2009). These protections (e.g., requiring informed consent, minimizing risks, verifying qualifications of those conducting the research) depend on the nature and location of the research.

Virtually all research conducted as part of a university, hospital, or government entity, or that is supported with public funds, is subject to review before it begins. In addition, many journals now require that research involving humans has been conducted pursuant to approval by an institutional review board (IRB). The IRB is obligated to consider the proposed study and ensure that human subjects receive adequate protection. There is a formal, sometimes complex, review process that includes especially careful consideration of the risks and benefits of the study, risks to particularly vulnerable populations (e.g., children, prisoners, mental health clients), and the informed consent subjects will receive (Resnik, 2004). The IRB may reject the study (seldom), approve it, or request modifications (common). The IRB has some obligations for continuing review while the study is under way. There are complaints that IRBs are too strict or not strict enough in their reviews, and that IRBs are unnecessary (Hoffman, 2003). They are very much a reality, however, for psychologists conducting research.

Psychologists conducting any study involving humans should expect to seek IRB review (Fiske, 2009). Many psychological studies will receive expedited review. In other circumstances, the review will be more extensive (Dresser, 2001). In clinical studies it is sometimes difficult to know what is research and what is just a modification of usual treatment approaches. Although there is no simple rule, if data are gathered for the purpose of obtaining results, the project is likely to be considered research, and if the treatment is a significant departure from accepted schools of thought, it may well be research or at least subject to special informed consent.

Failure to obtain IRB approval, or to conduct studies in accordance with professional standards, may have several legal consequences. It can result in liability for injuries that occur, for example. In most instances it would be a violation of university or other institutional policies and may lead to disciplinary action against the principal investigator.

Any psychologist considering undertaking research that involves human subjects should consult with colleagues who have experience, within the institution if possible (DuBois, 2008). Most IRBs offer considerable assistance to researchers, and contacting the IRB office is wise. These processes can take some time, so an early start on the process is important.

DEFAMATION

In essence, *defamation* is the publication of a falsehood about another person in a way that harms that person. Historically it has been divided into *slander,* which is an oral falsehood, and *libel,* which is written (including pictures). *Publication* in defamation is broadly defined to mean almost any communication to one or more persons. Suppose a psychologist tells Person A that she (the psychologist) believes that Person B is mentally ill and dangerous. If the statement is false and the psychologist has no basis for making it, this is defamation regardless of whether Person A or Person B is a client of the psychologist.

Defamation is in large part a reputational tort, so successful plaintiffs may recover damages for harm done to their reputations and emotional harm, as well as proven financial harm. Some communications are so likely to cause damages to another person that they are considered *per se defamation* and the plaintiff may be relieved of the obligation to show actual damages. Claims of serious crimes or allegations of mental illness, for example, have traditionally been *per se* defamation.

In professional psychology practice, defamation may appear in two forms. In one form, a client sues a therapist for publishing (i.e., communicating to at least one other person) a harmful false statement. An example would be a therapist who wrongfully sends to an employer a note that "Person X is paranoid and could easily become dangerous" when that is not true. Claims of defamation are fairly common because it is often a "tag on" (i.e., added on) to any claim of breach of confidentiality. Especially when psychologists did not have legal authority to be discussing a client at all, anything false or even misleading can appear to be defamatory. A psychologist who publishes an article about a client but enhances the story with untrue claims, for example, may be defaming the client if others can "unmask" who the individual is.

The second form of defamation is when one professional makes harmful and untrue statements about another professional. For example, if Person B falsely says to a potential employer that "Dr. C is not licensed and practices in an unethical way," Person B has defamed Dr. C and there are likely to be substantial damages for loss of reputation; loss of income; and, possibly, emotional suffering. An example of just such a case of defamation is discussed in the "Forensic Work" section later in this chapter.

There are many defenses to a claim of defamation, including the well-known defense of truth. In addition to common law defenses, there are significant First Amendment (free speech, freedom of the press) issues, so the U.S. Supreme Court has imposed many limitations on defamation. This makes the tort especially difficult to use successfully and the law enormously complex. Discussion of public officials, figures, and issues carries particular protection under the Constitution, and they have an especially difficult time proving defamation.

Claims of defamation may be excluded from coverage by a provider's malpractice insurance coverage. The therapist should be aware of such limitations in coverage and exercise care in releasing any information about clients.

CIVIL RIGHTS LIABILITY

There are many civil rights statutes, but the federal law most often referred to as creating civil rights liability is Section 1983 of the U.S. Code, "Civil Action for Deprivation of Rights." Section 1983 imposes civil liability on anyone who deprives another of civil rights while acting "under color of state law." This provision is of particular interest to professionals who work in state institutions or provide state services because they are, by definition, acting under color of state law. For example, a therapist who is involved in the civil commitment process or is providing treatment for prisoners may be depriving someone of liberty. To give rise to liability, however, the violation of federal rights has to be clear and unambiguous (Parry & Drogin, 2007).

In prison treatment cases, ordinary malpractice is insufficient to support liability under a Section 1983 claim. "Deliberate indifference" to the prisoner's medical needs is required. Someone who is clearly psychotic, banging his head against a wall, but who receives no attention from prison authorities could represent a case of deliberate indifference on the part of the authorities. On the other hand, one of the authors (David L. Shapiro) was involved in a case in which an inmate sued a department of corrections under a Section 1983 claim, maintaining that he had been misdiagnosed by prison officials and therefore was not receiving proper treatment. He had been diagnosed by the prison psychologist as having antisocial personality disorder. The inmate contended that his accurate diagnosis was borderline personality disorder and that he should therefore receive intensive individual psychotherapy. The court dismissed the case in favor of the defendant, holding that this was not deliberate indifference.

There are, of course, any number of other civil rights laws that prohibit discrimination based on race, sex, age, disability, and the like. Psychologists in their own practices must ensure that they abide by these requirements. In addition, there are many civil rights venues in which psychologists can work productively. They may assist in investigating possible violations, mediating complaints of violations, advising organizations or governments on ways of improving implementation of these rights, and testifying in court concerning disputes related to civil rights. There are considerable differences among the civil rights statutes. In each of these roles, psychologists need to understand specifically the role they are playing and some of the details of the civil rights law.

FORENSIC WORK

Forensic psychology requires special expertise and raises issues unlike those of other areas of practice (Greenberg, Shuman, Feldman, Middleton, & Ewing, 2007). Both attorneys who commonly hear forensic testimony and clinicians who practice forensic psychology regularly have seen an increased amount of forensic practice by individuals who have very limited forensic experience. The reason for this is unclear, although some have speculated that the shrinking marketplace and the economic difficulties of therapists caused by managed care have prompted many of them to stake out a niche in forensic practice (Shapiro, Walker, Manosevitz, Peterson, & Williams, 2008).

We have noted in several places the special considerations of forensic psychology practice. Any psychologist undertaking forensic work who is not very familiar with such practice should approach forensic assignments with great care and expect to spend substantial time preparing to do this work. Standard 2.01 of the APA Ethics Code, "Boundaries of Competence," provides some guidelines in this regard. Attending seminars and training sessions can be of considerable benefit, assuming they are well done. In addition, reading any of the several good handbooks for forensic practice is helpful. Consulting informally at least with one or two experienced forensic practitioners is also helpful.

When taking on a specific forensic assignment, it is important to be clear on what one's role will be (e.g., witness, consultant, decision maker). It is also important to have a reasonable understanding of the law that affects the forensic work to be done (Gutheil & Brodsky, 2010). If an attorney is engaging the psychologist, the psychologist should arrange for a detailed discussion of all of these matters; ideally, this will occur before a formal engagement is agreed to. Any such agreement should be in writing.

Heilbrun (1992) suggested using only assessment instruments that have a reasonable level of demonstrated validity for the purpose of forensic assessment. Some psychologists may claim that their clinical interview techniques are sufficient, but at a minimum psychologists need to demonstrate that these clinical techniques are documented and accepted in the professional and scientific literature. Indeed, the current Federal Rules of Evidence, as well as many states, now require demonstration of reliability of expert opinion presented at trial (Federal Rules of Evidence, Rule 702, 2010). (*Reliability*, as used in rules of evidence includes what psychologists would consider *validity* as well as *reliability*.) For instance, in evaluating the threat of potential violence it would be important to look at solid research, such as that done by the MacArthur Foundation, notably Monahan and Steadman's (1994, 2001) volumes. Their research has resulted in the identification of more than 30 domains or risk factors relevant to the potential for future violence. Using these domains as a guideline when conducting an assessment would demonstrate an adherence to a standard of care based on the most recent and relevant research. Other approaches have collapsed these factors into 20 dimensions (Webster, Douglas, Eaves, & Hart, 1997). Still others are purely actuarial approaches, based on weighted risk factors (Rice, Quinsey, & Harris, 1998). Again, the important fact is not so much which of these risk assessment approaches one uses but that one consistently and diligently uses an approach based on current research and documents it.

No area of forensic practice can match child custody evaluations in regard to misunderstanding, emotion, dissatisfaction, ethics complaints, and general hostility (Benjamin, Andrew, & Gollan, 2003; O. B. Caudill, 2006). It is common for states to give examiners providing testimony in such matters immunity from legal action if the statements are made in good faith (Binder, 2002). In *Obos v. Scripps Psychological Associates* (1997) a psychologist was conducting a child custody evaluation and was told that Obos (the boyfriend of the mother) had been dishonorably discharged from military service and fired from his job for dishonesty. The psychologist discussed these allegations with the therapist who was seeing the children as well as with the children's attorney. The allegations turned out to be untrue, and Obos sued the psychologist conducting the evaluation for defamation and invasion of his privacy. The court found that judicial immunity protected the psychologist, and stated, "We will not hamstring a court-appointed psychologist's efforts to ascertain the best environment for children by permitting such individuals subsequently to sue the psychologist for alleged [violations]." In short, the court recognized the necessity for a custody evaluator to examine all aspects of the case, including unsupported allegations, in order to do a complete and comprehensive evaluation without fear of a later lawsuit (O. B. Caudill, 2006).

Perhaps the most distressing forensic-related litigation is between therapists themselves. These frequently involve allegations of unethical conduct by one practitioner against another. In some cases there appears to be personal animus or an economic motivation. An especially expensive example is *Bizub v. Patterson* (2008), a case in which what the court referred to as an "unlicensed psychologist" sued a psychologist for defamation, among other things. Elizabeth Patterson (the defendant) sent letters to people for whom Marlene Bizub (the plaintiff) had worked, claiming that she had failed to report known cases of child abuse, was incompetent, misrepresented her credentials, and had been removed from cases. Patterson had filed four complaints to the state licensing board, all of which were dismissed. Patterson then allegedly told people that Bizub was under investigation by the board, all the while knowing that the complaints had been dismissed. Bizub claimed that as a result of these letters, lawyers stopped hiring her, even though they did not believe the allegations, in order to avoid any controversy. Bizub prevailed and was awarded $1.45 million in compensatory and punitive damages.

MEDICARE, INSURANCE, AND REIMBURSEMENT

Psychologists who receive Medicare, Medicaid, private insurance, or other reimbursement are subject to a wide range of laws. The passage of the federal mental health parity laws (Mental Health Parity and Addiction Equity Act of 2008) may expand the amount of reimbursement available to cover the care of some mental health clients, thereby increasing the necessity that therapists establish compliance programs to ensure that they meet the requirements of the law.

Reimbursement laws do not create traditional malpractice liability, but the consequences of not complying with the requirements of these laws can lead to substantial civil liability and even criminal penalties. A discussion of the laws surrounding reimbursement is well beyond the scope of this volume, but an example may make the point. The federal False Claims Act (2009) provides for civil damages and more when the federal government is charged for services not provided or that were provided in an inadequate or low-quality way. The government can enforce this law, but it also allows private citizens or whistleblowers (interveners) to bring an enforcement action on behalf of the government and keep part of the recovery. Thus, former employees, dissatisfied staff, and so on, may raise False Claims Act cases. Any psychologist receiving federal reimbursement, or substantial private insurance, for services should consult with attorneys or knowledgeable accountants to set up procedures to ensure compliance with the myriad laws that will be triggered by participation in these programs.

PHARMACEUTICALS

A major difference between malpractice claims in psychiatry and psychology is related to prescription drugs (Frank, Gupta, & McGlynn, 2008). For example, in recent times prescription antidepressants have been a frequent target of litigation, and often the prescribing psychiatrist is included as a defendant. If and when psychologists are granted prescribing privileges and commonly write prescriptions, their malpractice liability outlook will change substantially (Johnson, 2009).

By definition, prescription drugs carry substantial risks, and there are many things that can go wrong with them. The standard of care is almost inevitably higher when the risk of things going wrong increases. Pharmaceutical liability may arise from prescribing the wrong medication or prescribing the wrong dosage (because of obtaining an inadequate health history, physical examination, and/or medical workup for the client), failure to provide adequate information to the client about the drug (informed consent), careless administration of the drug, failure to monitor the client when a drug is known to have significant side effects, and overprescribing dangerous or controlled drugs (Frank et al., 2008). The standard of care may well be defined by all those with prescribing authority, not psychologists alone.

SPECIAL ISSUES IN TREATING CHILDREN
AND ADOLESCENTS

The treatment of children and adolescents requires a special understanding and experience (Tuckman & Ferro, 2004). Psychologists who hold themselves out as having special expertise are likely to be held to a specialized standard of care (see Standard 5.01, "Avoidance of False or Deceptive Statements," in the APA Ethics Code). In addition to the clinical expertise required for this work, working with children entails a number of signifi-cant legal issues. Many of these issues come down to questions of consent, information, and responsibility (Petti & Salguero, 2005).

Children have traditionally been legally incapable of consenting to treatment; only their parents can give consent (Prout & Prout, 2007). There are several exceptions to this traditional rule. *Emancipated minors* (those married, in the armed services, or living completely apart from their parents), for example, may give consent. Some state statutes specif-ically give minors authority to consent to certain kinds of care, including mental health services (McGuire & Bruce, 2008).

Where parents must give consent, difficulties may arise if the parents are divorced and one parent wants the child to be seen in therapy while the other party does not. Under such circumstances, a prudent practi-tioner should always ask to see the court papers to determine who has legal custody and can therefore make treatment decisions for the minor chil-dren. This does not apply, of course, to emergency situations in which a child needs to be seen immediately. The emergency intervention, how-ever, needs to be short lived, and the other parent must be informed of the treatment intervention. When there is joint legal custody, and both par-ents have equal rights in making decisions regarding medical and psycho-logical care, the situation can be complicated (Prout & Prout, 2007).

Such a situation was adjudicated in *Miller v. Board of Psychologist Examiners* (2004). The Oregon Board of Psychologist Examiners sanc-tioned Dr. Miller, a psychologist, for continuing to provide psychotherapy to two minor children after the father, who had recently been divorced from the mother, demanded that Miller stop seeing the children. The board determined that Miller had an ethical duty to provide psychotherapy only with the informed permission of a person legally authorized to grant that permission. The court of appeals overruled the board's finding and held in favor of Miller. The initial referral to Miller came about because Child Pro-tective Services staff had become concerned that the children may have been sexually abused. The social worker advised the mother to find a ther-apist for the children. The mother was the custodial parent and did give permission to Miller to see her children. Approximately 2 months into the treatment, the father, through his attorney, demanded that Miller stop seeing the children. Miller tried to contact both the father and his attorney, but neither responded to her. She sought ethical advice from two colleagues, both of whom told her that she needed to continue seeing the children. When the father filed a complaint with the Board of Psychologist Examiners, Miller then stopped seeing the children in therapy. Miller did the appropriate things when confronted with an ethical dilemma: She consulted with colleagues and documented the consultation. She initially obtained informed consent from the custodial parent. She then sought consultation and documented the consultation when problems arose.

Whether or not parents are required to consent to treatment of minor children, a separate issue arises regarding the access parents may have to information about their children from therapy (Petti & Salguero, 2005). Whenever possible, rules about the confidentiality of information should be clearly established with the parents and the child client before therapy begins (O. B. Caudill, 2006).

PRACTICAL SUGGESTIONS

1. Sexual misconduct remains a major cause of successful malpractice actions. Sexual contact with clients is malpractice and unethical. Don't do it.
2. For therapists falsely accused of sexual misconduct, be sure to document what the client said, how you responded, your consultation with a peer, and how you systematically followed up the situation.
3. Innovative or nontraditional therapies require special caution. Full disclosure and enhanced informed consent become especially important.
4. Psychologists conducting any human study should expect to seek IRB review and should consult with colleagues, within the institution if possible, who have experience in conducting research that requires IRB approval.
5. Defamation may arise from comments about clients or fellow professionals. Be cautious in making public statements about clients, and be very cautious about making derogatory statements about other psychologists.

6. Section 1983 of the U.S. Code imposes civil liability on anyone who deprives another of civil rights while acting "under color of state law." Psychologists who work for state entities should understand the nature of Section 1983 liability.

7. Psychologists who undertake forensic work should approach forensic assignments with great care and expect to spend a substantial amount of time preparing to do this work.

8. Psychologists who receive federal reimbursement, or substantial private insurance, for services should consult with attorneys or knowledgeable accountants to establish procedures to ensure compliance with the myriad laws that will be triggered by participation in these programs.

8

The Trial Process and Privileges

Malpractice cases come to conclusion through trial (sometimes) or settlement (usually). In this chapter, we discuss the process of a malpractice case from opening to appeal, and the alternative of settlement. Throughout this process the therapist–client testimonial privilege is of great importance, and we consider it in detail.

THE PROCESS OF A MALPRACTICE CASE

The civil claim process often begins with a *letter of demand* from the plaintiff(s) to the defendant(s). The more formal process begins when the plaintiff files with the court a *civil complaint.* The complaint sets out the basic claims and facts of the plaintiff's case. The defendant's reply to the complaint sets out the basics of the defense's view of the case. The claims in these initial pleadings may be changed during the course of the proceedings (Bogie & Marine, 2009).

Over the course of the following months or years, the judge will meet with the attorneys in the case; there will be preliminary motions regarding the case; and *discovery,* during which each side will seek relevant information from the other and from expert witnesses, will occur (Pope & Vasquez, 2005c). Three basic forms of discovery are: (a) written interrogatories (questions), (b) demands for the production of records, and (c) oral depositions. In *depositions,* parties and potential witnesses are asked questions, usually by the opposing counsel. During or after this time of discovery, a trial date is set, and the defense will usually move to dismiss the case (e.g., by making a motion for *summary judgment*). It is common for judges to push for settlement during this time or have the sides engage in mediation or other settlement-related talks (Sales, Miller, & Hall, 2005).

When the case goes to trial, it may be decided by a judge or a jury; that is, the *trier of fact* may be a judge or jury, usually depending on whether both parties agree to try it to the judge. If a jury is used, both sides question potential jurors (or provide questions for the judge to ask), and each side may challenge some jurors for *cause* (bias of some kind) or through a limited number of *peremptory strikes* (when jurors are eliminated by one side or the other). After the jury is selected, the opening statements of the plaintiff and the defendant are given, followed by a presentation of evidence. The plaintiff presents her or his case first, calling witnesses for direct examination, followed by cross-examination by the defense. After the plaintiff's case has been presented, the defense presents its case. There may be rebuttal testimony, and the attorneys make closing arguments. The judge then *charges* the jury, explaining the relevant law and the standards by which to make a judgment. The jury deliberates, then announces its verdict, which is either for the defendant (no recovery) or for the plaintiff with a dollar amount set by the jury. When there is a trial by the judge alone (called a *bench trial*), the judge serves as the "jury."

The judge may reverse or revise the jury's verdict if he or she views it as unreasonable. The parties (i.e., plaintiff and defendant) may appeal to a higher court to overturn the decision of the trial court, asserting that it was legally unacceptable. There are a number of bases for appeal, including the assertion that the judge incorrectly applied the law, made an error in instructions to the jury or misapplied the rules of evidence in a manner disadvantageous to one of the parties, or that the verdict was unreasonable. The appeals court may sustain or overturn the trial court and send it back to the trial court. Further appeals to higher courts are possible.

THE REALITY OF SETTLEMENT

The process of civil litigation usually results in settlement, not trial (Galanter & Cahill, 1994). Settlement may occur at any time, from before a complaint is filed to after appeal. Settlement avoids the uncertainty and expense of trial. (Even with discovery, the outcome of a trial may be a surprise.) Settlement also permits parties to structure the outcome of the case in a way that is consistent with their interests. Barkai, Kent, and Martin (2006) determined that of the 17 million civil cases filed in federal and state courts, 8 million were in state court, less than 3% of these reached a trial verdict, and less than 1% resulted in jury trials. Thus, 97% of cases were resolved without a trial. (These data were for 2003 cases.)

Courts encourage settlement in the name of efficiency. Settlement conferences, under the direction of a judge, are a common part of the process leading to trial. Many states either encourage or require that the parties to a suit engage in mediation prior to trial (Peters, 2007).

THE REALITY OF INSURANCE

Another major reality of malpractice cases is the central role played by insurance companies. Professional liability policies provide that the insurer will "defend and indemnify" the mental health professional in the event of a liability claim covered by the insurance policy (Pope & Vasquez, 2005b); that is, the insurance company will pay for the attorneys, court costs, experts, and the like and will pay (to the policy's limits) the cost of any judgment against the professional. Not all lawsuits, however, are covered by the insurance. For example, the insurance policy generally must have been in force when the claim was filed and when the events that are the subject of the suit occurred. Mental health coverage often excludes certain conduct, such as sex with clients (Roberson, 2001).

The professional is obligated to inform the insurance company of any legal notices that pertain to possible liability. Failure to do so may result in losing the coverage for the suit. The insurance company will ordinarily select the attorney to defend the case. For the most part the interests of the company and the professional are consistent: They both seek an inexpensive, successful and quick resolution to the case. It is possible for their interests to diverge, however. For example, the insurance company may wish to settle the case to avoid the cost of trial, but the professional may seek to avoid any suggestion of fault or wrongdoing by settling. (Some malpractice policies avoid such disputes by requiring that both the professional and the insurance company agree to any settlement.) When there is a substantial disagreement between insurance companies and professionals, the latter may need to consider obtaining private counsel, at their own expense, to protect their interests (Pope & Vasquez, 2005a).

In the United States, the rule of thumb is that each side pays its own attorneys' fees. In many other countries, the prevailing party's fees are paid by the losing side. A few statutes have changed the "American Rule" and instead allow the prevailing side, or at least one side, to be paid its attorneys' fees. Civil rights laws commonly allow the plaintiff to be awarded attorneys' fees if the plaintiff prevails but do not allow the same benefit to the defendants. A major advantage of insurance is that it pays attorneys' fees. Given the American Rule, without insurance, a defendant who wins can still pay enormous amounts for attorneys' fees for the preliminary motions, discovery, and if it goes that far, trial and appeal.

TESTIMONIAL PRIVILEGE

It is a general principle of law that every person must, when called on to do so, provide testimony that is relevant to cases that courts are deciding. An exception is *testimonial privilege,* which exists to protect some highly important communications that might not occur at all if they were not protected by a privilege. The law recognizes that some communications are very important to social interests and that those communications would probably not occur openly without special protection. Attorney–client, husband–wife, and therapist–client privileges are examples. The communications of therapy are frequent issues in malpractice cases, so the extent of the privilege is of considerable concern.

Privileges protect information from disclosure in court as well as in depositions and in other preliminary legal processes. They ordinarily also protect information from regulatory and legislative bodies. When the client is not competent, the holder of the privilege may be a guardian, a conservator, or a personal representative, although this varies from state to state. It is unclear whether the privilege survives the death of the client, but the trend appears to be against postmortem recognition of the privilege. Regardless of the status of the privilege after the death of the client, the ethical obligation to maintain client confidentiality remains even after death.

States are free to define for themselves what privileges apply in state court proceedings. All states provide for some form of a psychotherapist–client privilege. The labels of the privilege (*therapist–client, psychologist–client, psychiatrist–patient*), extent of the privilege, and exceptions to the privilege all vary from one state to another. As a general proposition, however, courts do not favor privileges because they remove relevant information that courts need to decide cases correctly. For that reason, courts tend toward a strict or narrow construction of privileges.

The place of the psychotherapist–client privilege in federal courts is somewhat complicated in the Federal Rules of Evidence. When federal courts apply state law (notably, in diversity-of-citizenship cases, where state law is applied in federal court because the citizen of one state has filed suit against a citizen of another state), they apply state privilege law. In federal court cases where federal law applies, federal common law determines whether there is a privilege. The U.S. Supreme Court has determined that in federal cases there is a common law therapist–client privilege (*Jaffee v. Redmond*, 1996).

In *Jaffee v. Redmond* (1996) the estate of a man killed by a police officer brought a lawsuit against the officer and the city. After the shooting, the police officer had numerous therapy sessions with a social worker. The plaintiff sought the therapy records, and the officer and therapist refused to provide them. The trial court, in its instructions to the jury, noted that the failure to provide the records should be considered in assessing the credibility of the defendant. On appeal, the U.S. Supreme Court held that a common law psychotherapist–client privilege existed in federal law and that it extended to communications between a client and his or her therapist (Odrobina, 2004).

The Court said that

> effective psychotherapy . . . depends upon an atmosphere of confidence and trust in which the patient is willing to make a frank and complete disclosure of facts, emotions, memories, and fears. Because of the sensitive natures of the problems for which individuals consult psychotherapists, disclosure of confidential communications made during counseling sessions may cause embarrassment or disgrace. (*Jaffee v. Redmond*, 1996, p. 10)

The Court added that "the psychotherapist privilege serves the public interest by facilitating the provision of appropriate treatment for individuals suffering the effects of a mental or emotional problem. The mental health of our citizenry is a public good of transcendent importance." The Court also recognized that all states have some form of therapist–client privilege and noted that the privilege is not absolute but is subject to exceptions. The Court declined to specify the exceptions but implied that the federal privilege would likely be subject to the same rules and exceptions that are common under state law (Buroker, 2004).

Thus, all states and the federal government recognize therapist–client privileges. Although the exact dimensions of the privileges vary from state to state, there are sufficient similarities to allow some generalizations.

Limits of the Privilege

In this section, we consider the many limitations on therapist–client privilege. These often substantially narrow the effective protection of confidentiality provided to clients.

Basic Requirements

Not every conversation with every therapist or counselor is privileged (Smith & Meyer, 1987). Therapist–client privilege comes into being only if the following three conditions are met:

1. The communication is with a licensed or certified professional as defined in the statute. States generally include in this category psychi-

atrists and psychologists, and many add social workers and certain counselors. These definitions usually include assistants to the professionals. The federal common law privilege includes a wide range of mental health professionals.

2. A professional relationship exists or is sought and the communication is related to professional services (Sydow, 2006). Informal communications are not privileged.

3. The communication is confidential. If the communication is revealed to another person—a friend, for example—confidentiality is compromised, and the privilege does not exist. At the extreme, it is possible that even the other members of group therapy or the transmittal of confidential information to insurance companies for reimbursement might be considered sufficient to destroy confidentiality and eliminate the privilege. The better view is that these communications remain privileged. There is no therapist–client privilege related to court-ordered examinations in either civil or criminal proceedings because there is no expectation of privacy. The client expects that the court and others will receive a copy of the report of the examination.

Assuming that communications meet all three of these conditions, there are a number of exceptions to the therapist–client privilege. Because of space limitations we deal here only with the more important, standard exceptions.

Voluntary Waiver

Clients may waive the privilege voluntarily. They may, for example, be anxious for the information from therapy to be available to courts because it is favorable or would be helpful. Waivers, however, are not generally partial. Once a client has decided to waive the privilege, all of the relevant information from therapy is subject to review in the court proceedings.

Client–Litigant Exception

Clients who bring their own mental condition into a legal controversy waive the privilege. The client–litigant exception is based on the concept that it would be unfair for the person to raise the issue of his or her own mental health and then use the privilege to hide relevant information.

The client–litigant exception frequently arises in malpractice cases. For example, say Client M files a malpractice suit against Dr. J, claiming that Dr. J misdiagnosed bipolar disorder, causing a delay in effective treatment, resulting in several months during which Client M missed work and suffered unnecessarily. Dr. J wishes to introduce all of his notes from therapy, but Client M refuses to waive the privilege. By filing a therapy malpractice claim, however, the client will almost always have waived the privilege. In this example, Client M will not be able to both maintain the malpractice claim against Dr. J and sustain the privilege.

This exception applies only when the client him- or herself has brought his or her own mental condition into a case; that is, the waiver of the privilege does not occur if the defense were to raise an issue about the mental health of the plaintiff (Boucher, 2007). Some courts, but not all, have decided that the client–litigant exception is waived whenever the plaintiff (client) claims emotional suffering. This exception to the privilege may put the client in the difficult position of abandoning a valid claim for damages or revealing the private communications in therapy (D. M. Smith, 2008). Clinicians should help ensure that a client who is in litigation has discussed with the attorney the exception to the privilege. Psychologists should not assume that the attorney, before referring the client, has fully discussed this matter.

Consider the following example case. A psychologist was referred a client for treatment of depression by her attorney. She had suffered a serious fall, which resulted in both physical and psychological injuries. She was suing the store on whose premises she fell, claiming that she had fallen because of some damaged stairs. She indicated, in response to the therapist's questions, that she had previously been treated with electroconvulsive therapy for depression. The therapist asked if she had discussed with her attorney the possibility that these hospital records could be subject to discovery because she had placed her mental state into litigation. She reported that her attorney had not mentioned this to her. The therapist suggested that she discuss this with her attorney. She did so and decided to drop the claim for mental and emotional injuries and focus on the physical injuries alone, feeling that she did not want to dredge up her history of previous emotional difficulties.

Dangerous-Client Exceptions

There are a couple of forms of dangerous-client exceptions to the privilege. The exceptions to confidentiality for child and other abuse reporting that we discussed in Chapter 4 generally also create privilege exceptions. Therefore, if something is required to be reported, it is likely not privileged. A number of states also create an "in need of hospitalization" exception, or eliminate privileges for civil commitment or when a person has made the kind of threat that would trigger a *Tarasoff* duty to protect (Parsio, 2007; see also Chapter 6, this volume).

Child Custody

Several states find a way of eliminating or waiving the privilege in child custody cases (Paruch, 2009). The theory behind this exception seems to be that the risk to the child of making an erroneous custody decision is so great that there cannot be a privilege when there may be important information from therapy that the court should have. States take several different approaches in regard to this (Grossman & Koocher, 2010). Some states preclude assertion of therapist–client privilege in custody matters, taking the position, noted earlier, that all mental health information concerning the parties in custody cases must be considered and that this includes any relevant therapy records (Stansbury, 2005). One version of this approach is to apply the client–litigant exception to any claim for custody. In other words, the mere act of seeking custody of a child is viewed as putting one's mental state into litigation because the mental and emotional fitness of the competing parties is a dimension to be considered by the judge. A better approach is that the custody dispute does not automatically waive privilege, but if certain claims regarding mental health become issues, then the privilege may be waived. For example, if one of the parents had made a recent suicide attempt, that would bring the mental health issue into consideration.

Other states take a different approach, holding that the therapist–client privilege is not waived in child custody cases. These states generally endorse the use of independent psychological evaluations to gain the relevant material instead of avoiding the protective privilege. Although not all practitioners are involved in custody litigation, the very complexity of the issues noted here should alert the practitioner to the fact that seemingly simple issues may in fact involve many complications. Before embarking on a particular kind of assessment, practitioners should review the regulations regarding what privileges apply to the particular situation, because they clearly vary from state to state.

Criminal Defense Exception

The existence of a possible "criminal defense exception" to the privilege is debated. The question is whether it is proper to withhold (from a criminal defendant) information from the therapy of a victim or witness that might exonerate the defendant. For example, suppose a victim in a rape case told her therapist that she consented to the sexual contact (*Commonwealth v. Fuller*, 1996). Should the defense have access to those therapy notes over the objection of the victim? States have taken different approaches to this issue. For contrasting viewpoints, see *Commonwealth v. Bishop* (1993), *Commonwealth v. Stockhammer* (1991), and *Goldsmith v. Maryland* (1993).

Exceptions and Confidentiality

Confidentiality exists whether or not a privilege is recognized or has been recognized (Bersoff, 2003). Even if no privilege exists, the therapist is still obligated to maintain confidentiality. Furthermore, even when a privilege is waived, other protections of confidentiality remain. For example, if the client–litigant exception exists regarding therapy, the mental health professional is not free to write an article using that information. There remain confidentiality obligations outside of the possible required testimony in court.

Relationship to the Attorney–Client Privilege

The interaction between the attorney–client privilege and therapist–client privilege can be complex. For example, even though no therapist privilege may exist for court-related examinations, when they are done to assist an attorney some of them may be covered by the attorney–client privilege. When issues arise in a forensic context, the psychologist should discuss the matter with the engaging attorney or the court, if the psychologist is court appointed.

The issue of attorney–client privilege generally exists in a criminal setting if a psychologist is doing an evaluation for a defense attorney. If the evaluation is being done for the state, it is likely that any material that is potentially of assistance to the defense needs to be revealed. If the evaluation is conducted pursuant to a court order, there may be less of a legal need for formal informed consent, although ethically it is advisable to obtain it.

Under such circumstances, a psychologist must inform the client as fully as possible regarding the parameters of the evaluation. The consent needs to be formulated in language that is reasonably understandable to the examinee. If the client is a minor or may be incompetent to give consent, the examination cannot proceed until such time as the court orders it or the defense gives appropriate consent.

WHAT IS A PSYCHOLOGIST TO DO?

When psychologists become involved with the legal system, they may, initially at least, feel they are a "stranger in a strange land." Whether a defendant in a lawsuit, the recipient of a subpoena, or a witness in court, the therapist should not act (or panic) without seeking trusted legal advice. It may be a strange land, but it can be managed with good advice and thoughtful action.

Being Sued

When psychologists receive a demand letter, complaint, or the like, they should immediately contact their attorney and then their insurance company. One of the reasons to have an ongoing relationship with an attorney is to reduce the possibility of a malpractice suit (Barnett & Johnson, 2008). Another reason is to have someone trusted to whom one can turn in the event of a claim or ethics complaint. An insurance company must be notified about a possible malpractice claim in a timely way, and the therapist's personal attorney can help make sure this is done properly. The insurance company should take over the defense of the claim. It may be helpful for the personal attorney to stay involved in a minor way to help explain the process and to provide a second opinion or protect the interests of the psychologist should there be a conflict with the insurance carrier.

Subpoenas

When therapists receive a subpoena about a client or former client, they should proceed with caution. They should not simply hand over the requested information but should consider matters carefully. The subpoena is not proof that revealing the information is legally permitted or required. It is usually a request for the information by the party opposed to the client. The subpoena may be part of an attorney's broad reach for information. Therapists should not reveal any records unless they receive the client's consent or it is otherwise clear that the information can be legally disclosed. The psychologist, for example, should ordinarily not try to determine themselves whether the client–litigant exception applies in the case (Matney, 1995).

The better approach is usually to contact the client, or former client, and ask for written instruction in regard to responding to the subpoena. That provides an opportunity for the client to challenge the release of information by seeking to quash the subpoena or otherwise challenge it. When in doubt about responding to what appears to be a court order, psychologists should contact their attorneys.

A special dilemma arises in the case of conjoint or group therapy, especially when the therapist keeps only one set of records for the group. Were a therapist to receive a subpoena for the records for such sessions, because one party has requested them, it could create a dilemma because none of the other group members (or their spouses) have waived the privilege. The therapist may need to seek agreement of the attorneys, or of the court, regarding ways of protecting the confidentiality of other members of the group while providing the information that can legitimately be released.

Stress and Strain

Everyone is upset when sued. Malpractice cases are particularly unnerving because they call into question one's professional competence and standing. The special stress and strain on mental health professionals and clients alike have been recounted in the literature (Kelley, 1996; Shapiro, Walker, Manosevitz, Peterson, & Williams, 2008). A mental health professional facing a malpractice claim will benefit from recognizing the stress and anger that such suits often entail.

For personal and professional reasons, as well as handling the legal issues as effectively as possible, professionals facing a malpractice claim should deal with their feelings directly, perhaps seeking the assistance of colleagues. They should establish good and open relationships with the attorneys representing them and recognize that processing the claim is likely to be extended and time consuming. Understanding the legal process and the steps along the way is a first step in dealing with a malpractice claim in the best possible way.

PRACTICAL SUGGESTIONS

1. If you receive a demand letter or legal complaint, immediately contact your personal attorney and notify your malpractice insurance carrier.
2. Malpractice policies provide that the insurer will "defend and indemnify" the mental health professional. The insurance carrier will ordinarily appoint defense counsel in a malpractice case. The psychologist should, early in the proceedings, establish a good working relationship with the attorney and come to an understanding about the approach to defending the action.
3. Psychologists facing a malpractice action should understand the legal landscape and timeline. It is appropriate to ask the attorney to explain the law related to the case and how the process will unfold. The preliminary process of demand letter, complaint, answer, and discovery can take many months.
4. It is more likely that a malpractice case will be settled rather than go to trial. Psychologists may request that the attorney keep them fully informed of the progress of settlement negotiations.

5. Therapist–client privilege is an important protection of the communications of therapy. Psychologists should understand the requirements of, and exceptions (there are many) to, the privilege.

6. Proceed with caution when a subpoena arrives concerning client records. The subpoena is not proof that revealing the information is legally permitted or required. Do not reveal any records unless the client has consented or it is otherwise clear that the information can be properly disclosed.

7. In the event of a malpractice claim, feelings of frustration, betrayal, and anger are to be expected. Deal with these feelings directly: Seek the assistance of colleagues; establish good relationships with the attorneys representing you; and understand that processing the claim is likely to be an extended, lengthy endeavor.

9

Risk Management Strategies and "Closing Arguments"

Everyone's grandmother was right: An ounce of prevention *is* worth a pound of cure—in malpractice, too. This chapter is about the ounce of prevention.

There is much clinicians can do to reduce both the amount of negligence in their practice and the number of malpractice claims they encounter (C. Miller, 2008). In this chapter, we look at both goals. There is no shortage of excellent suggestions for reducing malpractice claims (Packman, Smith, & Andalibian, 2007). After reviewing broad categories of risk management, we give our top suggestions for avoiding negligence and malpractice claims.

SOLID PROFESSIONAL PRACTICE

Throughout this volume we have stressed the necessity of defining and adhering to a professionally acceptable standard of practice. The essence of most negligence claims is that a deviation from a standard of care caused harm (Sales, Miller, & Hall, 2005). It follows that adherence to the relevant standard of care is the best protection against a successful malpractice action. The increased availability of formal standards of practice will make it easier to discern those assessment and treatment approaches that clearly do not meet professional standards. At the same time, research on the causation of emotional injuries and on malingering will help both mental health practitioners and the legal system to distinguish real from spurious claims.

Claiming Expertise

Practitioners and the profession as a whole need to be cautious about claiming expertise that does not exist. In terms of professional expertise, the worst position for a profession to be in regarding malpractice is to have oversold itself (S. R. Smith, 1991). This appeared to happen in the prediction of dangerousness, where mental health professionals have for years, under oath, predicted dangerousness in civil commitment, capital sentencing, and custody cases (Slobogin, 2007). It is now difficult for mental health professionals to claim that they should not be held liable for failing to predict dangerousness (e.g., *Tarasoff v. Regents of the University of California, 1976*) because they cannot make such determinations (Monahan, 2008). S. R. Smith (1991) described this as a "petard liability"—that is, mental health professionals are basically hoisting themselves on their own claims of expertise. For individual practitioners, claiming to have an expertise, or holding oneself out as having it, usually means that the law will hold the practitioner to actually having that special expertise. Some level of humility by practitioners and the profession itself is justified.

Ethical Codes and Other Professional Guidelines

Ethical principles and codes of conduct are important in malpractice cases and in risk management. Being familiar with the content of such documents, and following them except for good cause is a good way to manage and reduce the risks of professional practice. Those documents may play a role, sometimes a critical role, in defining the standard of care in malpractice cases (Shuman, 1997).

Much of the American Psychological Association's (APA's; 2010) "Ethical Principles of Psychologists and Code of Conduct" (http://www.apa.org/ethics/code/index.aspx), for example, set a minimal standard for practice. The standards in this document are deliberately phrased in a manner that allows them to be applied to all areas of practice. While the broad Principles embodied in the Ethics Code are aspirational in nature, the Ethical Standards themselves are enforceable and therefore are important sources of expected conduct and practice.

Some of the frequently cited areas in the APA Ethics Code relevant to malpractice actions are

- obtaining informed consent to professional services,
- practicing within the boundaries of one's competence,
- avoiding harmful multiple relations,
- maintaining confidentiality,
- explaining to clients the limits of confidentiality when they exist,
- avoiding harm and exploitation,
- basing opinions on sufficient data,
- avoiding misrepresentation of one's services, and
- making sure that one's practice is based on established professional and scientific standards.

Practice Standards

In addition to the APA Ethics Code there are a variety of standards that inform practice in various areas. For example, the American Educational Research Association, American Psychological Association, and National Council on Measurement in Education's (1999) "Standards for Educational and Psychological Testing" define the parameters of appropriate use of psychological assessments. In addition, a variety of guidelines have been published that help to define good practice and aspirational goals of a given field. These include the APA "Specialty Guidelines for Forensic Psychologists" (APA Committee on Ethical Guidelines for Forensic Psychologists, 1991), the APA (2007) "Record Keeping Guidelines", and the APA (1994) "Guidelines for Child Custody Evaluations in Divorce Proceedings." These guidelines help define a model of desirable professional practice. They are not standards of care in and of themselves but are seen as part of the level of practice of the average professional. Competent practitioners should be familiar with these documents and generally attempt to keep their practice in accordance with them.

These documents are very important because they help to define appropriate practices and avoid any "Monday morning quarterbacking." It is helpful for therapists to be able to say that they adhered to established standards or guidelines. These guidelines also help prevent some of the more outrageous testimony presented by self-proclaimed "experts" in the field. The promulgation of documents that describe the current state of the art in assessment of the potential for future violence, for example, could be very helpful in countering testimony that has no scientific basis.

Good practice also requires that psychologists keep up to date on the research in all of their areas of practice. This information should include assessment of violent behavior and of suicidal behavior, proper diagnostic procedures, and proper therapeutic techniques. Of course, there may well be a wide variety of such techniques, but the practitioner should be able to reference certain widely accepted techniques and procedures from peer-reviewed research and professional practice documents.

Cautious Innovation

The recommendation that one be able to cite scientific and professional literature that supports the treatments one uses need not mean that practice should be rigid and unchanging. Advances in professional practice require innovative approaches and techniques; however, practitioners who develop such new assessments or techniques must undertake such experimentation with caution. They should document sound bases for the departure from standard practice, protect clients fully, obtain informed consent tailored to the innovative treatment, and seek regulatory approval where appropriate.

The APA Ethics Code, in discussing competence, acknowledges that some areas of psychology do not have any recognized standards for training, and in such areas clinicians must exercise special caution to avoid causing harm to the client. For instance, the area of practice involving recovered memories of child sexual abuse has been very controversial. For that reason responsible practitioners have developed techniques that minimize the likelihood that the therapist will inadvertently create false recovered memories. Techniques such as hypnosis, age regression, and sodium amytal are strongly discouraged.

If a new technique is used, then a client should be given full informed-consent information about the new procedure. The specific consent will depend on the nature of the procedure and how great a departure it is from standard practice. In any event, the client should clearly be informed of any experimental technique and have the opportunity to opt out of it.

Consultation

Many malpractice cases have a hidden mistake: the failure to consult a colleague about a tough situation. In the case of Dr. Richter (a psychiatrist in Colorado who was sued by a client with whom he had had a sexual relationship), a critical series of questions to the doctor from the plaintiff's attorney had to do with the fact that he had never sought professional consultation when he felt sexually attracted to a client (*Roberts-Henry v. Richter,* 1990). Consultation should be well documented because it shows that the therapist is seeking to verify that her or his behavior meets the standard of care by checking with colleagues. Consultations are essential when a therapist is treating a high-risk client (e.g., one who has a potential for violence, including suicide) or has a concern regarding impaired judgment or personal issues (e.g., countertransference), uncertainty about diagnosis, or an issue of abuse. If referring a client to a colleague is not desirable for some reason, consultation is essential when therapists are treating clients with whom, or encounters situations with which, they have had limited or no training. Therapists should create records with the expectation that the client will have access to them and will be reading them.

Documentation

Although inadequate or nonexistent documentation of assessment and treatment is not a cause of action in malpractice, the quality of documentation can have a major impact in a malpractice action. It is important for practitioners to document how they reached a diagnosis and how that was translated into an appropriate therapeutic intervention. A well-documented record is one of the best defenses in a malpractice action or, for that matter, in licensing board complaints (Shapiro et al., 2008; Soisson, Vandecreek, & Knapp, 1987). No matter how skillful or intuitive a particular practitioner may be, "if it is not written down, it did not happen."

Stromberg (1988) noted that "detailed records usually help rather than hurt a health care professional in defending against claims; sloppy, sparse records appear unprofessional, uncaring, haughty, or deceptive" (p. 487). If, for example, a client consents to treatment and later states that she was treated without consent, the therapist's notes will be essential in proving the consent. On the other hand, the lack of adequate discharge notes is illustrated by *Davis v. Lhim* (1983). In this case, the psychiatrist did not document any discussion of the seemingly threatening statements the client made to his mother in the emergency room, making it look as though the psychiatrist had ignored the threat. Had the psychiatrist indicated that these statements were the product of drug-induced agitation and that there was no behavior consistent with the threatening statements, this may have reduced the likelihood that the subsequent lawsuit would be successful.

APA revised its Record Keeping Guidelines in 2007, making them far more detailed than the 1993 version. The guidelines suggest that a chart contain certain identifying data regarding the client, the type of service provided, dates of service, important actions taken, diagnosis, insurance and fee information, informed-consent documents, treatment plans, and progress notes. The APA Ethics Code states that it is unethical to withhold records because the client has not paid the bill if the records are for some reason required (Barnett & Johnson, 2008).

Virtually all state licensing boards have provisions in their administrative code that speak to the necessity of keeping adequate records. Therapists should be able to demonstrate, on the basis of their assessment, why they chose a particular intervention or course of treatment instead of another. In short, psychotherapy records are an essential aspect of professional survival in an age of litigation. Notes have to be meaningful and directly track the treatment plan.

Some therapists believe in keeping two sets of records: (a) an official set of progress notes, which, in the case of litigation, they would reveal; and (b) a private set of process notes that reveals their hunches, speculations, and dynamic formulations. The Health Insurance Portability and Accountability Act of 1996 (HIPAA) recognizes psychotherapy notes that receive special treatment under that statute. It is unlikely, however, that this second set of notes is completely exempt from legal discovery. Progress notes are legally discoverable, as are other records, and a request for "all of the records related to therapy" probably requires production of these notes along with the rest of the records.

An inexperienced therapist may well ask how anyone would ever become aware of the second set of notes. There are several ways. For example, at a deposition the therapist will inevitably be asked a question: "Now, Doctor, are these records you have produced all of the records of any sort that you have created or kept regarding Client X?" Perjury, of course, is not a satisfactory option, so the second set of records would have to be revealed. The case of *Lozano v. Bean-Bayog* ("*Lozano v. Bean-Bayog* settled," 1992) involved a therapist who believed that she could protect the private records. In that case the therapist was treating a seriously disturbed young man with a somewhat innovative treatment. She believed that it was essential to keep track not only of the client's verbalizations and her responses but also of her thoughts, dreams, and countertransference fantasies about the client. She believed that these were protected by keeping them in a private file that she believed was immune from legal discovery. The client eventually committed suicide, and the therapist was sued. The plaintiff's attorneys demanded all records, and the court ultimately compelled disclosure of these records. The revelation of this set of private notes became very embarrassing for the therapist. She settled the case out of court and surrendered her license (Chafetz, 1995).

Record keeping is also complicated at present by HIPAA. The HIPAA Privacy Rule permits special protection of confidential mental health information. As we suggested in Chapter 4, HIPAA, as amended in 2009 via the Health Information Technology for Economic and Clinical Health Act, is so complex that it is unwise for psychologists to establish their own record-keeping practices and informed consent as well as other forms. Legal assistance is necessary.

Records Retention

An important issue is how long records need to be retained after the termination of professional contact. This varies depending on the state, the nature of the professional service, and the like. Some general guidance is possible, but therapists should establish formal record retention policies. APA (2007) suggested retention of the full record for 7 years and in the case of minors, 3 years from the age of majority, whichever one is longer. (APA previously suggested 3 years for the full record and that summaries be kept for an additional 12 years; APA, 1993.)

Forensic records pose a number of additional considerations. In forensic work, because cases may be relitigated or appealed, it is wise to keep as much of the record as is necessary to anticipate questions that may come up on subsequent appeals. Never destroy records that could become subject to litigation. Particularly in criminal cases, the possibility of postappeal proceedings (notably *habeas corpus,* by which convicted individuals seek release from incarceration) argues for keeping many forensic records beyond the 7 years following the apparent end of litigation. It may be wise to discuss record retention with an attorney.

Clients often demand copies of their actual therapy charts, and under HIPAA they are entitled to them, unless the psychologist believes it would harm the client. Often, a summary may satisfy the client. Canter, Bennett, Jones, and Nagy (1994) suggested that the following should be included in summaries: client's presenting complaint and its history; consultations; referrals; diagnoses; treatment plans; medications; progress notes; psychological assessments; and if applicable, termination notes.

BEST OF ALL: AVOIDING CLAIMS

In addition to the technical requirements of negligence, ordinarily something else (an aggravating factor) is present before a malpractice claim is filed (Simon & Shuman, 2009). The absence of good communication, failure to respect an injured client, and dishonesty are likely to create an atmosphere in which a malpractice claim is more likely to be filed. For some clients, the claim is a way to find out the truth about what happened (Meruelo, 2008). For others, it is an effort to make sure that similar harm does not occur with future clients. Some clients have a strong sense of being wronged and believe that nobody has been held responsible for the wrong (S. R. Smith, 1991).

Mental health professionals' close relationships with clients undoubtedly contribute to the comparatively low number of malpractice claims. At the same time, there is a special sense of betrayal when a mental health professional has acted unprofessionally. Therapists may be able to use the natural relationship with clients to avoid formal claims when the harm has been unintentional and an honest mistake.

The place of apology and accepting responsibility for health care mishaps has been hotly debated (MacDonald & Attaran, 2009). We believe that such apologies, if honest, are professionally appropriate and likely to reduce the claims actually filed (Robbennolt, 2010). The argument on the other side has been that such apologies can constitute confessions and may be admitted in evidence against the professional should a malpractice suit go to trial. The majority of states have adopted *apology statutes* that allow health professionals and others to apologize for errors without those apologies being used as evidence against the professional (Robbennolt, 2008). These are positive developments, and mental health professionals who are facing the consequences of errors should consider the benefits of such apologies.

TOP WAYS TO AVOID NEGLIGENCE AND MALPRACTICE CLAIMS: A SUMMATION

We conclude with our "Top Principles" for, first, decreasing the potential of negligent practice and, second, avoiding malpractice claims against any mental health practitioner.

1. Adhere to good, professional practice. Ultimately, malpractice is professionally unacceptable practice.

2. Practice only within the bounds of your competence, defined conservatively (i.e., areas in which you have knowledge, skill, experience, education, and training). Conduct a careful self-analysis of your areas of expertise; accept referrals only in your areas of competence.

3. Know the literature, and be up to date in any area in which you practice.

4. Document fully and carefully all aspects of client care. Keep records consistent and up to date.

5. Understand, read periodically, and follow formal codes of ethics and practice guidelines in your areas of practice.

6. Establish standard office procedures to provide for documentation and accurate record keeping. Comply with such legal requirements as HIPAA, the Americans with Disabilities Act of 1990, and abuse-reporting laws.

7. Maintain client confidentiality. Be aware of the legal constraints that are operating and the relevant issues regarding privilege, confidentiality, and informed consent.

8. Obtain good, thorough consent that is truly informed and reflects true communications with the client.

9. Undertake innovative or experimental assessment or treatment with care. Ensure that such innovation is based on solid research, has special informed consent, complies with all ethical rules, and has necessary regulatory (institutional review board) approval.

10. Use care in selecting and supervising assistants.

11. When supervising another professional, take seriously the legal and ethical obligations that flow from this relationship. Do not engage in "phantom supervision."

12. Make sure that matters that could be particularly troublesome, such as a client showing an intense interest in the therapist's private life, are discussed in treatment and fully documented in the record, including consultation where appropriate.

13. When concerns arise about potential suicide, make sure there is a well-documented, comprehensive assessment that follows an estab-

lished model. Appropriate interventions should follow from this assessment and should be modified if the assessment changes. Be sure to document changes if they occur.

14. If clients make believable threats against others, take actions to avoid serious injury or death. If there is an identifiable intended victim, consider a specific warning to that person, or take other steps to protect the intended victim.

15. Exercise great care in terminating clients' therapy or transferring them to another provider. It is important never to appear to be abandoning a client without an effective referral or other ethical and effective termination of the therapy relationship.

16. Never hold yourself out as having a specialization or special expertise, training, or experience that you do not have.

17. If you are engaged in forensic work, understand the special limitation and obligation of this practice. Do not undertake forensic work without understanding how this work may change the usual relationship with clients and impose special obligations and responsibilities.

18. Maintain appropriate boundaries; do not mix roles or engage in potentially harmful multiple relationships.

19. Never engage in sexual contact with a client. Sexual contact with a former client should also be avoided.

20. Use only well-validated assessment and treatment techniques. Use the parameters outlined in an accepted instrument, and address each of the specified dimensions.

21. Maintain good relationships with clients; be flexible and open regarding their concerns. Know who the client is. Consider the value of apology and of accepting responsibility when an error has caused an injury.

22. Deal with fee collection in a cautious manner. If there have been difficulties or problems with a client, aggressive fee collection may trigger a malpractice action.

23. Maintain liability insurance that covers fully your practice. Seek risk-reduction advice from your insurance carrier.

24. If you receive a demand letter related to your practice, consult your insurance carrier and your attorney immediately.

25. Work with an attorney on an ongoing basis to practice preventive law by structuring your practice in a way that minimizes malpractice risks. Have annual "checkups" with the attorney to keep up to date and ensure that there is an ongoing risk reduction program.

A FINAL NOTE

Our final word is a plea to the professions of psychology and law. The nature of malpractice drives professions apart. The threat of malpractice is distressing to any professional, and the focus of this book invites an antagonism between the mental health professions and the legal profession. Such antagonism is unhealthy for both professions and for the clients we serve. So, our plea is for cooperation between the mental health professions and legal profession. Whether working with the needs of individuals in resolving problems and disputes; establishing codes of ethics and practice standards; or working on public policy matters, regulations, or statutes, the two professions should find ways of working together routinely.

There are a number of dedicated leaders in both professions who are undertaking just such cooperative efforts. Their work is important, and our hope is that malpractice law will be one area in which the law improves as a result of the cooperative spirit.

References

Abraham v. Zaslow, No. D-1330, N 374, (Cal. App. Super Ct. No. 245862 1975).

Addington v. Texas, 441 U.S. 418 (1979).

Alexander, G. J., & Scheflin, A. W. (1998). *Abraham v. Zaslow*. In *Law and mental disorder* (pp. 208–210). Durham, NC: Carolina Academic Press.

Allbright, A., Levy, F., & Wagle, N. C. (2002). Outpatient civil commitment laws: An overview. *Mental and Physical Disability Law Reporter, 26,* 179–182.

Alliance of Psychodynamic Organizations. (2006). *Psychodynamic diagnostic manual.* Silver Spring, MD: Alliance of Psychoanalytic Organizations.

American Association of Marriage and Family Therapists. (2001). *Code of ethics.* Retrieved from http://www.aamft.org/resources/lrm_plan/ethics/ethics code2001.asp

American Educational Research Association, American Psychological Association, & National Council on Measurement in Education. (1999). *Standards for educational and psychological testing.* Washington, DC: American Educational Research Association.

American Psychiatric Association. (2000). *Diagnostic and statistical manual of mental disorders* (4th ed., text revision). Washington, DC: Author.

American Psychiatric Association. (2009). *The principles of medical ethics, with annotations especially applicable to psychiatry* (2009 revised ed.). Arlington, VA: Author. Retrieved from http://psych.org/mainmenu/psychiatricpractice/ethics/ resourcesstandards/principlesofmedicalethics.aspx

American Psychological Association. (1993). Record keeping guidelines. *American Psychologist, 48,* 984–986.

American Psychological Association. (1994). Guidelines for child custody evaluations in divorce proceedings. *American Psychologist, 49,* 677–680. doi:10.1037/0003-066X.49.7.677

American Psychological Association. (1996). *Violence and the family: Report of the American Psychological Association presidential task force on violence and the family.* Washington, DC: Author.

American Psychological Association. (2002). Ethical principles of psychologists and code of conduct. *American Psychologist, 57,* 1060–1073.

American Psychological Association. (2006). Evidence-based practice in psychology. *American Psychologist, 61,* 271–285.

American Psychological Association. (2007). Record keeping guidelines. *American Psychologist, 62,* 993–1004. doi:10.1037/0003-066X.62.9.993

American Psychological Association. (2010). *Ethical principles of psychologists and code of conduct* (2002, amended June 1, 2010). Washington, DC: Author. Retrieved from http://www.apa.org/ethics/code/index.aspx

American Psychological Association. Committee on Ethical Guidelines for Forensic Psychologists. (1991). Specialty guidelines for forensic psychologists. *Law and Human Behavior, 15,* 655–665. doi:10.1007/BF01065858

American Psychological Association. Committee on Legal Issues. (2006). Strategies for private practitioners coping with subpoenas or compelled testimony for client records or test data. *Professional Psychology: Research and Practice, 37,* 215–222.

American Psychological Association. Committee on Psychological Tests and Assessment. (1996). Statement on the disclosure of test data. *American Psychologist, 51,* 644–648.

American Psychological Association Practice Organization. (2009). *Getting ready for the HIPAA privacy rule: A primer for psychologists.* Washington, DC: Author. Retrieved from http://www.American Psychological Associationpractice central.org/business/hipaa/2009-privacy.pdf

Americans With Disabilities Act of 1990, 42 U.S.C. § 12101 *et seq.*

Americans With Disabilities Amendments Act of 2008, Pub. L. No. 110-325, 122 Stat. 3553.

Appelbaum, P. S. (1996). Legal liability and managed care. *American Psychologist, 48,* 251–257.

Ash, P. (2010). Principles and practice of child and adolescent forensic mental health. In E. P. Benedek, P. Ash, & C. L. Scott (Eds.), *Malpractice and professional liability* (pp. 419–429). Arlington, VA: American Psychiatric Publishing.

Association of State and Provincial Psychology Boards. (2005). *Code of conduct.* Peachtree City, GA: Author. Retrieved from http://asppb.org/publications/model/conduct.aspx

Austin, K. M., Moline, M. E., & Williams, G. T. (1990). *Confronting malpractice: Legal and ethical dilemmas in psychotherapy.* Thousand Oaks, CA: Sage.

Baerger, D. R. (2001). Risk management with the suicidal patient: Lessons from case law. *Professional Psychology: Research and Practice, 32,* 359–366.

Baker v. United States, 226 F. Supp. 129 (S.D. Iowa #1964).

Barkai, J., Kent, E., & Martin, P. (2006). A profile of settlement. *Court Review: The Journal of the American Judges Association, 42,* 34–39.

Barnett, J. E., & Johnson, W. B. (2008). Responding to an ethics complaint, licensure board complaint, or malpractice suit. In *Ethics desk reference for psychologists* (pp. 201–203). Washington, DC: American Psychological Association.

Barratt, E. S. (1965). Factor analysis of some psychometric measures of impulsiveness and anxiety. *Psychological Reports, 16,* 547–554.

Beck, J. (1990). Clinical aspects of the duty to warn or protect. In R. I. Simon (Ed.), *Review of clinical psychiatry and the law* (Vol. 1, pp. 191–204). Washington, DC: American Psychiatric Press.

Behnke, S. H. (2000). Suicide, contributory negligence, and the idea of individual autonomy. *Journal of the American Academy of Psychiatry and the Law, 28,* 64–73.

Behnke, S. H. (2004, November). Release of test data and the new ethics code. *Monitor on Psychology, 35*(10), 90–91.

Behnke, S. H., Perlin, M. L., & Bernstein, M. D. (2005). *Tarasoff* and the duty to protect. *NYS Psychologist, 17,* 21–26.

Behnke, S., Winick, B., & Perez, A. (1999). Confidentiality, Testimonial Privilege, and Mandatory Reporting. *Essentials of Florida mental health law* (pp. 146–149). New York, NY: Norton.

Belar, C. D., & Deardorff, W. W. (2009). Liability risks in clinical health psychology: Malpractice claims and licensing board complaints. In *Clinical health psychology in medical settings: A practitioner's guidebook* (2nd ed., pp. 191–234). Washington, DC: American Psychological Association.

Bellah v. Greenson, 146 Cal. Rptr. 535 (1st Dist. 1978).

Bender, L. (2003). *Bender visual–motor gestalt test* (2nd ed.). Oxford, England: Pearson Assessment.

Benjamin, G., Andrew, H., & Gollan, J. K. (2003). *Family evaluation in custody litigation: Reducing risks of ethical infractions and malpractice.* Washington, DC: American Psychological Association. doi:10.1037/10593-000

Benjamin, G. A. H., Kent, L., & Sirikantraporn, S. (2008). A review of duty-to-protect statutes, cases, and procedures for positive practice. In J. L. Werth, Jr., E. R. Welfel, & G. A. H. Benjamin (Eds.), *The duty to protect: Ethical, legal, and professional considerations for mental health professionals* (pp. 229–247). Washington, DC: American Psychological Association.

Bennett, B. E., Bricklin, P. M., Harrs, E., Knapp, S., VandeCreek, L., & Younggren, J. N. (2006). *Assessing and managing risk in psychological practice: An individualized approach.* Rockville, MD: The Trust.

Bennett, B., Bryant, B., VandenBos, G., & Greenwood, A. (1990). *Professional liability and risk management.* Washington, DC: American Psychological Association. doi:10.1037/11102-000.

Berg, J., Appelbaum, P., Parker, L., & Lidz, C. (2001). *Informed consent: Legal theory and clinical practice.* New York, NY: Oxford University Press.

Berman, A. L. (2006). Risk management with suicidal patients. *Journal of Clinical Psychology, 62,* 171–184.

Berman, A. L., Jobes, D. A., & Silverman, M. M. (2006). Standards of care and malpractice in suicide treatment. In *Adolescent suicide: Assessment and intervention* (2nd ed., pp. 259–286). Washington, DC: American Psychological Association.

Bersoff, D. N. (1981). Testing and the law. *American Psychologist, 36,* 1047. doi:10.1037/0003-066X.36.10.1047

Bersoff, D. N. (Ed.). (2003). *Ethical conflicts in psychology* (3rd ed.). Washington, DC: American Psychological Association.

Bersoff, D. N. (Ed.). (2008). *Ethical conflicts in psychology* (4th ed.). Washington, DC: American Psychological Association.

Bigler, E. (1981). The continued inappropriate singular use of the Bender Visual–Motor Gestalt Test. *Professional Psychology, 12,* 562–569. doi:10.1037/0735-7028.12.5.562

Binder, R. L. (2002). Liability for the psychiatrist expert witness. *American Journal of Psychiatry, 159,* 1819–1825. doi:10.1176/appi.ajp.159.11.1819

Bingham v. Lifespring, No. 82-5128 (E.D. Pa. July 31, 1984), reported in 28 ATLA Rep. 139 (1985).

Bizub v. Patterson, No. 07-CV-1960 (Colo. Dist. Ct. 2008).

Bloom, J. D. (2004). Thirty-five years of working with civil commitment statutes. *Journal of the American Academy of Psychiatry and the Law, 32,* 430–439.

Blum, D. (1986). *Bad karma: A true story of obsession and murder.* New York, NY: Antheum.

Bogie, M. A., & Marine, E. C. (2009). Civil lawsuits: Malpractice professional liability claims process and claims history. In S. F. Bucky, J. E. Callan, & G. Stricker (Eds.), *Ethical and legal issues for mental health professionals in forensic settings* (pp. 141–163). New York, NY: Routledge/Taylor & Francis Group.

Bongar, B. (2002). Legal perspectives. In *The suicidal patient: Clinical and legal standards of care* (2nd ed., pp. 39–80). Washington, DC: American Psychological Association. doi:10.1037/10424-002

Borum, R. (2009). Children and adolescents at risk of violence. In P. M. Kleespies (Ed.), *Behavioral emergencies: An evidence-based resource for evaluating and managing risk of suicide, violence, and victimization* (pp. 147–163). Washington, DC: American Psychological Association.

Boucher, A. O. (2007). Implied waiver of physician and psychotherapist–patient privilege in North Dakota medical malpractice and personal injury litigation. *North Dakota Law Review, 83*, 855–885.

Bowermaster, J. M. (2002). Legal presumptions and the role of mental health professionals in child custody proceedings. *Duquesne Law Review, 40*, 68–117.

Brady v. Hopper, 570 F. Supp. 1333 (D. Col. 1983) aff'd 751 F.2d 329 (10th Cir. 1984).

Bruch, C. S. (2001). Parental alienation syndrome and parental alienation: Getting it wrong in child custody cases. *Family Law Quarterly, 35*, 572–552.

Bucky, S. F., Callan, J. E., & Stricker, G. (2009). *Ethical and legal issues for mental health professionals in forensic settings.* New York, NY: Routledge/Taylor & Francis.

Buroker, D. M. (2004). The psychotherapist–patient privilege and post-*Jaffee* confusion. *Iowa Law Review, 89*, 1373–1389.

Caesar v. Montanos, 542 F.2d 1064 (9th Cir. 1976).

Caddy v. Florida Department of Health, Board of Psychology, 764 So.2d 625 (Fla. Dist. Ct. App. 2000).

Calfee, B. E. (1998). Risk management realities surface in new practice environment. In R. F. Small & L. R. Barnhill (Eds.), *Practicing in the new mental health marketplace: Ethical, legal, and moral issues* (pp. 227–238). Washington, DC: American Psychological Association. doi:10.1037/10271-012

Canadian Psychological Association. (2000). *Canadian code of ethics for psychologists* (3rd ed.). Ottawa, Ontario, Canada: Author.

Canon v. Thumudo, 422 N.W.2d 688 (Mich. 1988).

Canter, M., Bennett, B., Jones, S. E., & Nagy, T. (1994). *Ethics for psychologists: A commentary on the American Psychological Association Ethics Code.* Washington, DC: American Psychological Association. doi:10.1037/10162-000

Canterbury v. Spence, 464 F.2d 772 (D.C. Cir. 1972).

Cardi, W. J. (2009). A pluralistic analysis of the therapist/physician duty to warn third parties. *Wake Forest Law Review, 44*, 877–897.

Carmichael v. Carmichael, 597 A.2d 1326 (D.C. 1991).

Caudill, O. B., Jr. (2001). Malpractice and licensing pitfalls for therapists: A defense attorney's list. In L. D. Vandecreek (Ed.), *Innovations in clinical practice: A source book (Vol. 20).* Sarasota, FL: Professional Resource Press.

Caudill, O. B., Jr. (2006). Avoiding malpractice in child forensic assessment. In S. N. Sparta & G. P. Koocher (Eds.), *Forensic mental health assessment of children and adolescents* (pp. 74–87). New York, NY: Oxford University Press.

Chafetz, G. S. (1995). *Obsession: The bizarre relationship between a prominent Harvard psychiatrist and her suicidal patient.* New York, NY: Random House.

Chodoff, P. (2005). Psychiatric diagnosis: A sixty year perspective. *Psychiatric News, 40,* 17–28.

Civil Action for Deprivation of Rights, 42 U.S.C. § 1983.

Cohen, R. J. (1979). *Malpractice: A guide for mental health professionals.* New York, NY: Free Press.

Commonwealth v. Bishop, 617 N.E.2d 990 (Mass. 1993).

Commonwealth v. Fuller, 667 N.E.2d 847 (Mass. 1996).

Commonwealth v. Stockhammer, 570 N.E.2d 992 (Mass. 1991).

Confidentiality of Alcohol and Drug Abuse Patient Records, Cal. Civ. Code § 43.92, 42 C.F.R. Part II, 2010.

Conn, S. B. (2009). Malpractice: "Open" discovery in the age of HIPAA. *Michigan Bar Journal, 88,* 27–33.

Cook, D. A. (2009). Thorough informed consent: A developing clinical intervention with suicidal clients. *Theory, Research, Practice, Training, 46,* 469–471.

Courtois, C. (1999). *Recollections of sexual abuse.* New York, NY: Norton.

Crawford, R. L. (1994). *Avoiding counselor malpractice.* Alexandria, VA: American Counseling Association.

Davis v. Lhim, 335 N.W.2d 481 (Mich. Ct. App. 1983).

Dawe v. Bar-Levav, 780 N.W.2d 272 (Mich. 2010).

DeJesus v. United States Department of Veteran Affairs, 479 F.3d 271 (3d Cir. 2007).

DeLettre, J. L., & Carter, S. L. (2010). Keeping psychotherapy notes separate from the patient record. *Clinical Psychology & Psychotherapy, 17,* 160–163.

D'Emanuele, R. C., Soshnik, J. T., & Bomash, K. (2009, June). Major changes to HIPAA security and privacy rules enacted in economic stimulus package. *Health Lawyers News,* 32–38.

Deming, A. (2008). Sex offender civil commitment programs: Current practices, characteristics, and resident demographics. *Journal of Psychiatry & Law, 36,* 439–461.

Doe v. High Tech Institute, Inc., 972, P. 2d 1060 (1998), No. 97CAO385, WL 379926 (Colo. Ct. App. 1998).

Doe v. Roe, 400 N.Y.S.2d 668 (Sup. Ct. 1977).

Dresser, R. (2001). Research participants with mental disabilities: The more things change. In L. E. Frost & R. J. Bonnie (Eds.), *The evolution of mental health law* (pp. 57–74). Washington, DC: American Psychological Association. doi:10.1037/10414-003

Drogin, E. Y. (2008). Sexual offender risk assessment tools: A jurisprudent science perspective. *Journal of Psychiatry & Law, 36,* 513–520.

DuBois, J. M. (2008). *Ethics in mental health research: Principles, guidance, and cases.* New York, NY: Oxford University Press.

Durney v. Terk, 840 N.Y.S.2d 30 (App. Div. 2007).

Ebert, B. W. (2006). *Multiple relationships and conflict of interest for mental health professionals: A conservative psychological approach.* Sarasota, FL: Professional Resource Press/Professional Resource Exchange.

Edwards, G. S. (2010a). *Database of state* Tarasoff *laws.* Retrieved from http://www.ssrn.com/abstract=1551505

Edwards, G. S. (2010b). *Doing their duty: An empirical analysis of the unintended effect of* Tarasoff v Regents *on homicidal activity* (Emory Law and Economics Research Paper No. 10-61). Retrieved from http://www.ssrn.com/abstract=1544574

Elliott v. North Carolina Psychology Board, 498 S.E.2d 616 (N.C. 1998).

Emergency Medical Treatment and Active Labor Act of 1994 (42 U.S.C. 1395, 1986).

Epstein, R. A. (1976). Medical malpractice: The case for contract. *American Bar Foundation Research Journal, 1,* 87–149.

Erard, R. E. (2004). Release of test data under the 2002 ethics code and the HIPAA privacy rule: A raw deal or just a half-baked idea? *Journal of Personality Assessment, 82,* 23–30. doi:10.1207/s15327752jpa8201_4

Estates of Morgan v. Fairfield Family Counseling Center, 673 N.E.2d 1311 (Ohio 1997).

Everstine, L., Everstine, D. S., Heymann, G. M., True, R. H., Frey, D. H., Johnson, H. G., & Seiden, R. H. (2008). Privacy and confidentiality in psychotherapy. In D. N. Bersoff (Ed.), *Ethical conflicts in psychology* (4th ed., pp. 166–168). Washington, DC: American Psychological Association.

Ewing v. Goldstein, 15 Cal. Rptr.3d 864 (Ct. App. 2004).

Exner, J. E., Jr. (2002). *The Rorschach: A comprehensive system* (Vol. 1). New York, NY: Wiley.

False Claims Act, 31 U.S.C. §§ 3729 et seq. (2009).

Federal Rules of Evidence, Rule 702 (2010).

Federal Tort Claims Act, 28 U.S.C., §§ 1346(b), 2761-2680 (2010).

Feldman, S. R., Moritz, S. H., & Benjamin, G. A. H. (2005). Suicide and the law: A practical overview for mental health professionals. In K. M. Weiner (Ed.), *Therapeutic and legal issues for therapists who have survived a client suicide: Breaking the silence* (pp. 95–103). New York, NY: Haworth Press.

Ferris, C. E. (2008). The search for due process in civil commitment hearings: How procedural realities have altered substantive standards. *Vanderbilt Law Review, 61,* 959–981.

Fiske, S. T. (2009). Institutional review boards: From bane to benefit. *Perspectives on Psychological Science, 4,* 30–31.

Florida Administrative Code § 64B19-16.003(1)

Frank, B., Gupta, S., & McGlynn, D. J. (2008). Psychotropic medications and informed consent: A review. *Annals of Clinical Psychiatry, 20,* 87–95.

Funk v. Feldman, 512 P.2d 539 (Kan. 1973).

Galanter, M., & Cahill, M. (1994). Judicial promotion and regulation of settlements. *Stanford Law Review, 46,* 1339. doi:10.2307/1229161

Gans, L. A. (1999). Inverts, perverts, and converts: Sexual orientation, conversion therapy and liability. *Boston University Public Interest Law Journal, 8,* 219–249.

Garber, S., Greenberg, M. D., Rhodes, H., Zhou, X., & Adams, J. L. (2009). Do noneconomic damages caps and attorney fee limits reduce access to justice for victims of medical negligence? *Journal of Empirical Legal Studies, 6,* 637–686. doi:10.1111/j.1740-1461.2009.01156.x

Garcia v. Santa Rosa Health Care Corporation, 925 S.W.2d 372 (Tex. Ct. App. 1996).

Gardner, R. (1972). *Parental alienation syndrome: A guide for mental health and legal professionals.* DeKalb, Ill: Creative Therapeutics.

Garvey, K. A., Penn, J. V., Campbell, A. L., Esposito-Smythers, C., & Spirito, A. (2009). Contracting for safety with patients: Clinical practice and forensic implications. *Journal of the American Academy of Psychiatry and the Law, 37,* 363–370.

Givelber, D., Bowers, W., & Blitch, C. (1984). *Tarasoff,* myth and reality: An empirical study of private law in action. *Wisconsin Law Review, 443,* 475.

Goldsmith v. Maryland, 651 A.2d 866 (Md. 1993).

Goldstein, A. M. (Ed.). (2003). *Forensic psychology: Vol. 11. Handbook of psychology.* Hoboken, NJ: Wiley.

Gordon, R. J. (1969). Mental distress in psychological research. *Baylor Law Review, 21,* 520–528.

Gorman, S. W. (2009). Sex outside of the therapy hour: Practical and constitutional limitations on therapist sexual misconduct regulations. *UCLA Law Review, 56,* 983–1039.

Greenberg, S. A., Shuman, D. W., Feldman, S. R., Middleton, C., & Ewing, C. P. (2007). Lessons for forensic practice drawn from the law of malpractice. In A. M. Goldstein (Ed.), *Forensic psychology: Emerging topics and expanding roles* (pp. 446–461). Hoboken, NJ: Wiley.

Griffin v. Twin Valley Psychiatric System, 771 N.E.2d 945, 118 Ohio Misc. 2d 301 (2002).

Grisso, T., & Appelbaum, T. (1998). *MacArthur Competence Assessment Tool for Treatment.* Sarasota, FL: Professional Resource Press.

Gross v. Allen, 27 Cal. Rptr. 2d 429 (2d Dist. 1994).

Grossman, L. R., & Koocher, G. P. (2010). Privacy, confidentiality, and privilege of health records and psychotherapy notes in custody cases. *American Journal of Family Law, 24,* 41–50.

Guedj, M., Sastre, M. T. M., Mullet, E., & Sorum, P. C. (2009). Is it acceptable for a psychiatrist to break confidentiality to prevent spousal violence? *International Journal of Law and Psychiatry, 32,* 108–114. doi:10.1016/j.ijlp.2009.01.003

Gutheil, T. G., & Brodsky, A. (2010). Commentary: *Tarasoff* duties arising from a forensic independent medical examination. *Journal of the American Academy of Psychiatry and the Law, 38,* 57–60.

Hales, R., Yudofsky, S., & Gabbard, G. (2008). *Textbook of psychiatry* (5th ed.). Arlington, VA: American Psychiatric Publishing.

Hall, R. C. W., & Resnick, P. J. (2008). Psychotherapy malpractice: New pitfalls. *Journal of Psychiatric Practice, 14,* 119–121. doi:10.1097/01.pra.0000314319. 87168.d7

Hamman v. County of Maricopa, 775 P.2d 1122 (Ariz. 1989).

Hammer v. Rosen, 165 N.E.2d 756 (N.Y. 1960).

Harley, E. M. (2007). Hindsight bias in legal decision making. *Social Cognition, 25,* 48–63. doi:10.1521/soco.2007.25.1.48

Health Information Technology for Economic and Clinical Health Act (HITECH). Pub. L. No. 111-5, 123 Stat. 524 (2009).

Health Insurance Portability and Accountability Act (HIPAA), Pub. L. No. 104-191, 110 Stat. 1936 (1996).

Health Insurance Portability and Accountability Privacy Rule, 45 C.F.R. §§ 160, 164(A)(E) (2010).

Health Insurance Portability and Accountability Security Rule, 45 C.F.R. §§ 160, 164(A)(E) (2010).

Hedges, L. E. (2007). *Facing the challenge of liability in psychotherapy: Practicing defensively* (3rd ed.). Lanham, MD: Jason Aronson.

Heilbrun, K. (1992). The role of psychological testing in forensic assessment. *Law and Human Behavior, 16,* 257–272. doi:10.1007/BF01044769

Helling v. Carey, 519 P.2d 981 (Wash. 1974).

Helinski v. Rosenberg, 616 A.2d 866 (Md. 1992)

Higgins v. Salt Lake County, 855 P.2d 231 (Utah 1993).

Hixson, R. (2005). Risky business. *Annals of the American Psychotherapy Association, 8,* 37–39.

Hoffman, S. (2003). Regulating clinical research: Informed consent, privacy, and IRBs. *Capital University Law Review, 31,* 71–91.

Hoffman v. Blackmon, 241 So.2d 752 (Fla. App. 1970).

Holroyd, J. C., & Brodsky, A. M. (1977). Psychologists' attitudes and practices regarding erotic and non-erotic physical contact with patients. *American Psychologist, 32,* 843–849. doi:10.1037/0003-066X.32.10.843

Huffman, M. K. (2008). Immunity and mental health professionals. *University of Dayton Law Review, 33,* 265–283.

Hung, E., & Chamberlain, J. (2009). Sexually violent predators and civil commitment proceedings. *Journal of the American Academy of Psychiatry and the Law, 37*, 266–268.

Hungerford v. Jones, 722 A.2d 478 (N.H. 1998).

Illingworth, P. M. L. (1995). Patient–therapist sex: Criminalization and its discontents. *Journal of Contemporary Health Law and Policy, 11*, 389–416.

Indiana v. Edwards, 554 U.S. 164 (2008).

Individuals With Disabilities Education Improvement Act of 2004, Pub. L. 108-446, 20 U.S.C. § 1400.

In re Lifschutz, 467 P.2d 557 (Cal. 1970).

Jaffee v. Redmond, 518 U.S. 1 (1996).

Jeffries v. McCague, 363 A.2d 1167 (Pa. Super. Ct. 1976).

Jobes, D. A., & O'Connor, S. S. (2008). The duty to protect suicidal clients: Ethical, legal, and professional considerations. In J. L. Werth, Jr., E. R. Welfel, & A. H. Benjamin (Eds.), *The duty to protect: Ethical, legal, and professional considerations for mental health professionals* (pp. 163–180). Washington, DC: American Psychological Association.

Johnston, M. (1997). *Spectral evidence: The Ramona case. Incest, memory, and truth on trial in NAmerican Psychological Association Valley*. Boston, MA: Houghton Mifflin.

Kachigian, C., & Felthous, A. R. (2004). Court responses to *Tarasoff* statutes. *Journal of the American Academy of Psychiatry and the Law, 32*, 263–273.

Kalichman, S. C. (1999). *Mandated reporting of suspected child abuse: Ethics, law and policy* (2nd ed.). Washington, DC: American Psychological Association. doi:10.1037/10337-000

Karasek v. LaJoie, 699 N.E.2d 889 (N.Y. 1998).

Karraker v. Rent-A-Center, 411 F.3d 831 (7th Cir. 2005).

Kelley, J. L. (1996). *Psychiatric malpractice: Stories of patients, psychiatrists, and the law*. New Brunswick, NJ: Rutgers University Press.

Kendell, R., & Jablonsky, A. (2003). Distinguishing between the validity and utility of psychiatric diagnosis. *American Journal of Psychiatry, 160*, 4–12. doi:10.1176/appi.ajp.160.1.4

Klinka, E. (2009). It's been a privilege: Advising patients of the *Tarasoff* duty and its legal consequences for the federal psychotherapist–patient privilege. *Fordham Law Review, 78*, 863–931.

Kohn, L. T., Corrigan, J. M., & Donaldson, M. S. (Eds.). (2000). *To err is human: Building a safer health system*. Washington, DC: National Academy Press.

Koocher, G., & Connell, M. (2003). HIPAA and forensic practice: Expert opinion. *American Psychology Law Society News, 23*(2), 16–19.

Lees-Haley, P. R., & Courtney, J. C. (2000). Disclosure of tests and raw data to the courts: A need for reform. *Neuropsychology Review, 10,* 169–174. doi:10.1023/A:1009031615267

Lemon v. Stewart, 682 A2d 1177 (Md. 1996).

Lewis, M. H., Gohagan, J. K., & Merenstein, D. J. (2007). The locality rule and the physician's dilemma: Local medical practices vs. the national standard of care. *Journal of the American Medical Association, 297,* 2633–2637. doi:10.1001/jama.297.23.2633

Long, A. B. (2008). Introducing the new and improved Americans with Disabilities Act: Assessing the ADA Amendments Act of 2008. *Northwestern University Law Review Colloquy, 103,* 217–229.

Lozano v. Bean-Bayog settled out of court. (1992). *Time.* Retrieved from http://www.time.com/time/magazine/articles/0.9171.975273.00.html

MacDonald, N., & Attaran, A. (2009). Medical errors, apologies and apology laws. *Canadian Medical Association Journal, 180,* 11. doi:10.1503/cmaj.081997

Marks v. Tenbrunsel, 910 So.2d 1255 (Ala. 2005).

Marshall v. Klebanov, 902 A.2d 873 (N.J. 2006).

Martin, K. R. (2007). Tort law: Third Circuit holds federal agency liable for deaths mentally-ill patient caused after negligent discharge from treatment program—*De Jesus v. United States Department of Veteran Affairs. American Journal of Law & Medicine, 33,* 527.

Matney, J. (1995). What's it worth? The patient–litigant exception whittles away at the physician–patient and mental health information privileges. *Texas Tech Law Review, 26,* 993–1011.

Matthews, J. L. (2003). *The lawsuit survival guide.* Berkeley, CA: Nolo Press.

McClellan, F. (2006). Medical malpractice law, morality and the culture wars: A critical assessment of the tort reform movement. *Journal of Legal Medicine, 27,* 33–53. doi:10.1080/01947640500533275

McGuire, A. L., & Bruce, C. R. (2008). Keeping children's secrets: Confidentiality in the physician–patient relationship. *Houston Journal of Health Law & Policy, 8,* 315–333.

Mental Health Parity and Addiction Equity Act of 2008, Pub. L. No. 110-343, 122 Stat. 3765 (2008).

Meruelo, N. C. (2008). Mediation and medical malpractice: The need to understand why patients sue and a proposal for a specific model of mediation. *Journal of Legal Medicine, 29,* 285–306. doi:10.1080/01947640802297553

Meyers, C. (1997). Expanding *Tarasoff:* Protecting patients and the public by keeping subsequent caregivers informed. *Journal of Psychiatry & Law, 25,* 365–375.

Milgram, S. (1974). *Obedience to authority: An experimental view.* New York, NY: HarperCollins.

Miller v. Board of Psychologist Examiners, 91 P.3d 786 (Or. Ct. App. 2004).

Miller, A. L., & Emanuele, J. M. (2009). Children and adolescents at risk of suicide. In P. M. Kleespies (Ed.), *Behavioral emergencies: An evidence-based resource for evaluating and managing risk of suicide, violence, and victimization* (pp. 79–101). Washington, DC: American Psychological Association.

Miller, C. (2008). Ethical and legal issues. In M. Hersen & A. M. Gross (Eds.), *Handbook of clinical psychology: Vol. 1. Adults* (pp. 95–109). Hoboken, NJ: Wiley.

Monahan, J. (1981). *The clinical prediction of violent behavior.* Thousand Oaks, CA: Sage.

Monahan, J. (2006). Tarasoff at thirty: How developments in science and policy shape the common law. *University of Cincinnati Law Review, 75,* 497–521.

Monahan, J. (2008). Limiting therapist exposure to *Tarasoff's* liability: Guidelines for risk containment. In D. N. Bersoff (Ed.), *Ethical conflicts in psychology* (4th ed., pp. 180–186). Washington, DC: American Psychological Association.

Monahan, J., & Steadman, H. (1994). *Violence and mental disorder.* Chicago, IL: University of Chicago Press.

Monahan, J., & Steadman, H. (2001). *Rethinking risk assessment.* New York, NY: Oxford University Press.

Moncrieff, A. R. (2009). Federalization snowballs: The need for national action in medical malpractice reform. *Columbia Law Review, 109,* 844–892.

Morey, L. C. (2007). *Personality Assessment Inventory professional manual.* Lutz, FL: Psychological Assessment Resources.

Morgan, C. D., Soetaert, D. K., & Heinrichs, R. J. (2008). Supervision in medical settings. In A. K. Hess, K. D. Hess, & T. H. Hess (Eds.), *Psychotherapy supervision: Theory, research, and practice* (2nd ed., pp. 450–470). Hoboken, NJ: Wiley.

Naidu v. Laird, 539 A.2d 1064 (Del. 1988).

Nash, N. C. (1986, June 1). Exploring strategies that work: Insiders' trading. *The New York Times,* p. 47.

National Association of Social Workers. (2008). *Code of ethics of the National Association of Social Workers.* Washington, DC: Author. Retrieved from http://www.naswdc.org/pubs/code/default.asp

N.O.L. v. District of Columbia, 674 A.2d 498 (D.C. 1995).

Obos v. Scripps Psychological Associates, 69 Cal. Rptr.2d 30 (Dist. Ct. App. 1997).

O'Connor v. Donaldson, 422 U.S. 563 (1975).

Odrobina, J. L. (2004). The lingering questions of a Supreme Court decision: The confines of the psychotherapist–patient privilege. *Cleveland State Law Review, 52,* 551–556.

O'Laughlin, M. J. (2001). Dr. Strangelove: Therapist–client dual relationship bans and freedom of association, or how I learned to stop worrying and love my clients. *UMKC Law Review, 69,* 697–731.

Olmstead v. L. C., 527 U.S. 581 (1999).

Orne, M. T. (1991, July 23). The Sexton tapes. *New York Times,* p. A21.

Oregon v. Miller, 709 P.2d 225 (Or. 1985).

Osheroff v. Chestnut Lodge, 490 A.2d 720 (Md. 1985).

Pabian, Y. L., Welfel, E., & Beebe, R. S. (2009). Psychologists' knowledge of their states' laws pertaining to *Tarasoff*-type situations. *Professional Psychology: Research and Practice, 40,* 8–14. doi:10.1037/a0014784

Packman, W., Andalibian, H., Eudy, K., Howard, B., & Bonger, B. (2009). Legal and ethical risk management with behavioral emergencies. In P. M. Kleespies (Ed.), *Behavioral emergencies: An evidence-based resource for evaluating and managing risk of suicide, violence, and victimization* (pp. 405–430). Washington, DC: American Psychological Association. doi:10.1037/11865-018

Packman, W., Smith, G., & Andalibian, H. (2007). Legal issues of psychiatric malpractice in suicide cases. *Directions in Psychiatry, 27,* 159–172.

Parham v. J.R., 442 U.S. 584 (1979).

Parry, J. (2010). *Civil mental disability law: Evidence and testimony.* Washington, DC: American Bar Association.

Parry, J., & Drogin, E. (2007). *Mental disability law: Evidence and testimony.* Washington, DC: American Bar Association.

Parsio, A. (2007). The psychotherapist–patient privilege: The perils of recognizing a "dangerous patient" exception in criminal trials. *New England Law Review, 41,* 623–659.

Paruch, D. (2009). The psychotherapist–patient privilege in the family court: An exemplar of disharmony between social policy goals, professional ethics, and the current state of the law. *Northern Illinois University Law Review, 29,* 499–570.

Patterson, W. W, Dohn, H., Bird, J., & Patterson, G. (1983). Evaluation of suicidal patients: The SAD PERSONS Scale. *Psychosomatics, 24,* 343–345, 348–349.

Peck v. Addison County Counseling Service, 499 A.2d 422 (Vt. 1985).

Perkes, C. (2007, December 7). Kaiser to pay $1.8 million in malpractice case. *Orange County Register.* Retrieved from http://www.ocregister.com/articles/blackwell-37247-pain-brain.html

Perreira v. State, 768 P.2d 1198 (Colo. 1989).

Peters, P. G., Jr. (2007). What we know about malpractice settlements. *Iowa Law Review, 92,* 1783–1833.

Petti, T. A., & Salguero, C. (Eds.). (2005). *Community child and adolescent psychiatry: A manual of clinical practice and consultation.* Arlington, VA: American Psychiatric Publishing.

Pincus, H. A., Zarin, D. A., & First, M. (1998). Clinical significance and *DSM–IV* [Letter to the editor]. *Archives of General Psychiatry, 55,* 1145. doi:10.1001/archpsyc.55.12.1145

Pope, K. S. (1994). *Sexual involvement with therapists.* Washington, DC: American Psychological Association. doi:10.1037/10154-000

Pope, K. S., & Brown, L. (1996). *Recovered memories of abuse: Assessment, treatment, forensics.* Washington, DC: American Psychological Association. doi:10.1037/10214-000

Pope, K. S., & Vasquez, M. J. T. (2005a). Finding an attorney. In *How to survive and thrive as a therapist: Information, ideas, and resources for psychologists in practice* (pp. 33–37). Washington, DC: American Psychological Association. doi:10.1037/11088-005

Pope, K. S., & Vasquez, M. J. T. (2005b). Finding professional liability coverage. In *How to survive and thrive as a therapist: Information, ideas, and resources for psychologists in practice* (pp. 39–45). Washington, DC: American Psychological Association. doi:10.1037/11088-006

Pope, K. S., & Vasquez, M. J. T. (2005c). Responding to a licensing, malpractice, or ethics complaint. In *How to survive and thrive as a therapist: Information, ideas, and resources for psychologists in practice* (pp. 87–93). Washington, DC: American Psychological Association. doi:10.1037/11088-011

Pope, K., & Vasquez, M. (2007). *Ethics in psychotherapy and counseling* (3rd ed.). San Francisco, CA: Jossey-Bass.

Poythress, N. G. (1990). Avoiding negligent release: Contemporary clinical and risk management strategies. *American Journal of Psychiatry, 147,* 994–997.

Prout, S. M., & Prout, H. T. (2007). Ethical and legal issues in psychological interventions with children and adolescents. In H. T. Prout & D. T. Brown (Eds.), *Counseling and psychotherapy with children and adolescents: Theory and practice for school and clinical settings* (4th ed., pp. 32–63). Hoboken, NJ: Wiley.

Ramona v. Isabella, No. 61898 (Cal. Super. Ct. May 13, 1994).

Rappleyea, D. L., Harris, S. M., White, M., & Simon, K. (2009). Termination: Legal and ethical considerations for marriage and family therapists. *American Journal of Family Therapy, 37,* 12–27. doi:10.1080/01926180801960617

Recupero, P. R. (2008). Clinical practice guidelines as learned treatises: Understanding their use as evidence in the courtroom. *Journal of the American Academy of Psychiatry and the Law, 36,* 290–301.

Recupero, P. R., & Rainey, S. E. (2005). Informed consent to e-therapy. *American Journal of Psychotherapy, 59,* 319–331.

Recupero, P. R., & Rainey, S. E. (2007). Liability and risk management in outpatient psychology supervision. *Journal of the American Academy of Psychiatry and the Law, 35,* 188–195.

Rehabilitation Act of 1973, Pub. L. No. 93-112, 29 U.S.C. 701-796 (2009).

Resnik, D. B. (2004). Liability for institutional review boards: From regulation to litigation. *Journal of Legal Medicine, 25,* 131–184. doi:10.1080/01947640490457451

Rice, M., Quinsey, V., & Harris, G. (1998). *Violent offenders: Appraising and managing risk.* Washington, DC: American Psychological Association.

Robbennolt, J. K. (2008). Attorneys, apologies, and settlement negotiation. *Harvard Negotiation Law Review, 13,* 349–397.

Robbennolt, J. K. (2010). Apologies and reasonableness: Some applications of psychology to torts. *De Paul Law Review, 59,* 489–513.

Roberson, L. M. (2001). Professional liability policies: Sexual misconduct limitations. *For the Defense, 43,* 35–40.

Roberts, A. R., Monferrari, I., & Yeager, K. (2008). Avoiding malpractice lawsuits by following risk assessment and suicide prevention guidelines. *Brief Treatment and Crisis Intervention, 8,* 5–14. doi:10.1093/brief-treatment/mhm029

Roberts-Henry v. Richter, 802 P.2nd 1159 (Colo. Ct. App. 1990).

Rogers, R., & Shuman, D. W. (2005). *Fundamentals of forensic practice: Mental health and criminal law.* New York, NY: Springer Science+Business Medica.

Rogge, S. (2000). Liability of psychiatrists under New York law for failing to identify dangerous patients. *Pace Law Review, 20,* 221–229.

Rosen, J. (1953). *Direct analysis.* New York, NY: Grune & Stratton.

Roth, E. J. (2009). Double secret: The unique confidentiality of substance abuse medical records. *Maine Bar Journal, 24,* 96.

Rudd, M. D., & Joiner, T. (1998). Assessment of suicidality: A framework for outpatient practice. In L. Vandecreek & T. Jackson (Eds.), *Innovations in clinical practice: A source book* (Vol. 17, pp. 1–17). Sarasota, FL: Professional Resource Press.

Runnels, M. B. (2009). Apologies all around: Advocating federal protection for the full apology in civil cases. *San Diego Law Review, 46,* 137–160.

Russell v. Adams, 482 S.E.2d 30 (N.C. Ct. App. 1997).

Saccuzzo, D. P. (1997). Liability for failure to supervise adequately mental health assistants, unlicensed practitioners and students. *California Western Law Review, 34,* 115–152.

Sales, B. D., Miller, M. O., & Hall, S. R. (2005). Liabilities for professional activities. In *Laws affecting clinical practice* (pp. 53–67). Washington, DC: American Psychological Association.

Sawyer v. Midelfort, 595 N.W.2d 423 (Wis. 1999).

Scope of psychiatrist's liability for acts of released inpatients: Colorado Supreme Court holds psychiatrist liable under negligent release theory for violent act of involuntarily committed mental patient. (1990). *Harvard Law Review, 103,* 1192–1198.

Sexual Misconduct in the Practice of Psychology, Florida Statute § 490.0111 (2010).

Shapiro, D., Walker, L., Manosevitz, M., Peterson, M., & Williams, M. (2008). *Surviving a licensing board complaint.* Phoenix, AZ: Zeig, Tucher & Theisen.

Sherer, R. A. (2007). Toward a twenty-first century civil commitment statute: A legal, medical, and policy analysis of preventive outpatient treatment. *Indiana Health Law Review, 4,* 1–74.

Shuman, D. W. (1997). The standard of care in medical malpractice claims, clinical practice guidelines, and managed care: Towards a therapeutic harmony? *California Western Law Review, 34,* 99–113.

Simmons v. United States, 805 F.2d 1363 (9th Cir. 1986).

Simon, R. I. (2006a). Clinically based risk management of the suicidal patient: Avoiding malpractice litigation. In R. I. Simon & R. E. Hales (Eds.), *The American Psychiatric Publishing textbook of suicide assessment and management* (pp. 545–575). Arlington, VA: American Psychiatric Publishing.

Simon, R. I. (2006b). The myth of "imminent" violence in psychiatry and the law. *University of Cincinnati Law Review, 75,* 631–644.

Simon, R. I., & Shuman, D. W. (2009). Therapeutic risk management of clinical–legal dilemmas: Should it be a core competency? *Journal of the American Academy of Psychiatry and the Law, 37,* 155–161.

Simone, S. J., & Fulero, S. (2001). Psychologists' perceptions of their duty to protect uninformed sex partners of HIV-positive clients. *Behavioral Sciences & the Law, 19,* 423–436. doi:10.1002/bsl.450

Slobogin, C. (2006). Dangerousness and expertise redux. *Emory Law Journal, 56,* 275–325.

Slobogin, C. (2007). *Proving the unprovable.* New York, NY: Oxford University Press.

Slovenko, R. (1998). Informed consent and defenses to a lack of informed consent. *Journal of Psychiatry & Law, 26,* 441–470.

Slovenko, R. (2005). Contributory fault of the patient in a malpractice action. *Journal of Psychiatry & Law, 33,* 291–307.

Smith, A. R., Witte, T. K., Teale, N. E., King, S. L., Bender, T. W., & Joiner, T. E. (2008). Revisiting impulsivity in suicide: Implications for civil liability of third parties. *Behavioral Sciences & the Law, 26,* 779–797. doi:10.1002/bsl.848

Smith, D. M. (2008). An uncertain privilege: Implied waiver and the evisceration of the psychotherapist–patient privilege in the federal courts. *De Paul Law Review, 58,* 79–151.

Smith, J. T. (1986). *Medical malpractice: Psychiatric care.* Colorado Springs, CO: Shepard's/McGraw-Hill.

Smith, S. R. (1986–1987). Medical and psychotherapy privileges and confidentiality: On giving with one hand and removing with the other. *Kentucky Law Journal, 75,* 473–557.

Smith, S. R. (1989). Mental health expert witnesses: Of science and crystal balls. *Behavioral Sciences & the Law, 7,* 145–180. doi:10.1002/bsl.2370070203

Smith, S. R. (1991). Mental health malpractice in the 1990's. *Houston Law Review, 28,* 209–282.

Smith, S. R. (1996). Malpractice liability of mental health professionals and institutions. In D. Shuman & B. D. Sales (Eds.), *Law, mental health, and mental disorder* (pp. 76–98). Belmont, CA: Thomson Brooks/Cole.

Smith, S. R. (2000). Malpractice. In A. E. Kazdin (Ed.), *Encyclopedia of psychology* (Vol. 5, pp. 99–100). Washington, DC: American Psychological Association/ Oxford University Press. doi:10.1037/10520-045

Smith, S. R., & Meyer, R. G. (1987). *Law, behavior and mental health: Policy and practice.* New York, NY: New York University Press.

Soisson, E., Vandecreek, L., & Knapp, S. (1987). Thorough record keeping: A good defense in a litigious era. *Professional Psychology: Research and Practice, 18,* 498–502. doi:10.1037/0735-7028.18.5.498

Sorrel, A. L. (2010, January). Liability by locality. *American Medical News, 25.*

Stansbury, C. (2005, May). Discovery of mental health records in custody disputes. *Family Law Review,* 1–16. Retrieved from http://www.gabar.org/public/pdf/ sections/familylaw/flsmay05news.pdf

State v. Watkins, 83 P.3d 1182 (Colo. Ct. App. 2003).

Strasburger, L. H., Jorgenson, L., & Randles, R. (2008). Criminalization of psychotherapist–patient sex. In D. N. Bersoff (Ed.), *Ethical conflicts in psychology* (4th ed., pp. 262–265). Washington, DC: American Psychological Association.

Stromberg, C. (1988). *The psychologist's legal handbook.* Washington, DC: National Register.

Suskind v. Lifespring, No. 83-4370 (E.D. Pa, November 19, 1984).

Sydow, N. (2006). A "shrink"-ing privilege: The course of diagnosis. Requirement of the psychotherapist–patient privilege. *Harvard Civil Rights–Civil Liberties Law Review, 41,* 265–275.

Tarasoff v. Regents of the University of California, 529 P.2d 553 (Cal. 1974).

Tarasoff v. Regents of the University of California, 551 P.2d 334 (Cal. 1976).

Tellefsen, C. (2009). Commentary: Lawyer phobia. *Journal of the American Academy of Psychiatry and the Law, 37,* 162–164.

Tellegen, A., Dahlstrom, G. Butcher, J. N., & Graham, J. R. (2001). *Minnesota Multiphasic Personality Inventory—2.* Oxford, England: Pearson Assessment.

Thayer v. OrRico, 792 N.E.2d 919 (Ind. Ct. App. 2003).

Thornwell v. United States, 471 F. Supp. 344 (D.D.C. 1979).

Till, G. J. (1993). Liability to others for the negligent release of an involuntary mental patient: Determining the law in Iowa. *Iowa Law Review, 78,* 1143–1167.

Tomlinson, E. O. (2009). Determining the medical and emotional bases for damages. *Medical Trial Technique Quarterly, 55,* 145–272.

Tracz v. Charter Centennial Peaks, 9 P.3d 1168 (Colo. Ct. App. 2000).

Travin, S., & Bluestone, H. (1987). Discharging the violent psychiatric inpatient. *Journal of Forensic Sciences, 32,* 999–1008.

Tsao, C. I., & Layde, J. B. (2007). A basic review of psychiatric medical malpractice law in the United States. *Comprehensive Psychiatry, 48,* 309–312. doi:10.1016/j.comppsych.2007.03.002

Tuckman, A. J., & Ferro, D. (2004). Professional liability and malpractice in adolescent psychiatry. *Adolescent Psychiatry, 28,* 59–75.

Turkat, I. D. (1995). Divorce related malicious mother syndrome. *Journal of Family Violence, 10,* 253–264.

United States v. Hayes, 227 F.3d 578 (6th Cir. 2000).

United States v. Willis, 737 F.Supp. 269, 272 (SDN.Y. 1990).

University of Minnesota, Human Rights Library. (2009). *United States V. Brandt (The medical case) Trials of war criminals before the Nuremberg military tribunals under control council law, No. 10 Vol. 2, at 181–182.* Available at http://www1.umn.edu/humanrts/instree/nuremberg.html

Vasquez, M. J. T., Bingham, R. P., & Barnett, J. E. (2008). Psychotherapy termination: Clinical and ethical responsibilities. *Journal of Clinical Psychology, 64,* 653–665. doi:10.1002/jclp.20478

Vaughn, K. S., & Gentry, G. K. (2006). Do no harm. In T. J. Vaughan (Ed.), *Psychology licensure and certification: What students need to know* (pp. 165–174). Washington, DC: American Psychological Association. doi:10.1037/11477-015

Wachler, A. B., & Fehn, A. K. (2009). The HITECH breach notification rules: Understanding the new obligations. *Health Lawyer, 22,* 36–60.

Walcott, D. M., Cerundolo, P., & Beck, J. C. (2001). Current analysis of the *Tarasoff* duty: An evolution towards the limitation of the duty to protect. *Behavioral Sciences & the Law, 19,* 325–343. doi:10.1002/bsl.444

Waller, G. (Producer). (2004). *Debating Richard Gardner* [DVD]. Seattle, WA: Intermedia, Inc. Available from http://www.intermedia-inc.com/title.asp?sku=DE06

Webster, C. D., Douglas, K. S., Eaves, D., & Hart, S. D. (1997). *HCR–20: Assessing the Risk for Violence* [Version 2]. Lutz, FL: Psychological Assessment Resources.

Webster, C. D., & Hucker, S. J. (2007). *Violence risk: Assessment and management.* Hoboken, NJ: Wiley.

Welch, B. (2000). *Reducing your suicide liability. Insight: Safeguarding psychologists against liability risks.* Amityville, NY: American Professional Agency.

Welfel, E. R. (2008). Emerging issues in the duty to protect. In J. L. Werth, Jr., E. R. Welfel, & G. A. H. Benjamin (Eds.), *The duty to protect: Ethical, legal and professional considerations for mental health professionals* (pp. 229–247). Washington, DC: American Psychological Association.

Werth, J. L., Jr., Welfel, E. R., & Benjamin, G. A. H. (2008). *The duty to protect: Ethical, legal, and professional considerations for mental health professionals.* Washington, DC: American Psychological Association.

Wexler, D. B. (2008). Two decades of therapeutic jurisprudence. *Touro Law Review, 24,* 17–29.

Wexler, D. B., & Schopp, R. F. (1989). How and when to correct for juror hindsight bias in mental health malpractice litigation: Some preliminary observations. *Behavioral Sciences & the Law, 7,* 485–504. doi:10.1002/bsl.2370070406

White v. United States, 780 F.2d 97 (D.C. Cir. 1986).

Whitree v. State, 290 N.Y.S.2d 486 (1968).

Wickline v. State of California, 239 Cal. Rptr. 810 (Cal. Ct. App. 1986).

Wiederholt v. Fischer, 485 NW.2d 442 (Wis. 1992).

Williamson v. Liptzin, 539 SE.2d 313 (N.C. Ct. App. 2000).

Wilson v. Blue Cross/Blue Shield of Southern California, 271 Cal. Rptr. 876 (Cal. Ct. App. 1990).

Woody, R. H. (2002). Clinical psychology in the courtroom: Part 1. Proper and multiple roles in forensic services. *Clinical Psychologist, 55,* 11–15.

Young, J. L., & Griffith, E. H. (1999). Developments in clergy malpractice: The case of *Sanders v. Casa View Baptist Church. Journal of the American Academy of Psychiatry and the Law, 27,* 143–147.

Youngberg v. Romeo, 457 U.S. 307 (1982).

Yufik, A. (2005). Revisiting the *Tarasoff* decision: Risk management and liability in clinical and forensic practice. *American Journal of Forensic Psychology, 23,* 5–21.

Zinermon v. Burch, 494 U.S. 113 (1990).

Zipkin v. Freeman, 436 SW.2d 753 (Mo. 1968).

Table of Authorities

Index

Standard of care
adherence to, 39
applying, 26–30
court application of, 80
jury understanding of, 40
proving, 30–33
structured instruments in, 99
Standards of practice, 153–160
and claims of expertise, 154
for consultations, 157
documentation in, 157–160
ethical codes in, 154–155
with innovations, 156–157
and legally recognizable injury, 14
professional guidelines for, 154–155
professionally accepted, 13–14
and records retention, 160
resources for, 155–156
State courts
jurisdictions of, 38
premature release cases in, 115–116
professional liability cases in, 8
testimonial privilege in, 143
tort cases in, 12
State institutions, 41
State laws
application of, in tort cases, 12
applied in federal courts, 143
on civil commitment, 110, 114–115
on civil rights, 129–130
confidentiality protections of, 62–63
and HIPAA requirements, 65
on informed consent, 54
on informed consent with
minors, 135
on liability, 19
on maximum awards, 23
on posttermination sexual
involvement, 121
on professional liability, 8
for reporting child abuse, 71–72
Tarasoff liability in, 107, 108
and U.S. Constitution, 113

on violent sex offenders, 111–112
on withholding records from
client, 67
State licensing boards, 158
Statement on the Disclosure of Test
Data, 69
Statute of limitations, 38
Steadman, Henry, 101, 132
Stock trading, 76
Strain/stress, 151
Strict liability, 16–17
Stromberg, Clifford, 158
Structured clinical judgment, 100
Structured settlements, 21
Subject matter jurisdiction, 38
Subpoenas, 150
Substantive defenses, 36
Suffering, 20, 39
Suicide, 97–104
Summary judgment, 140
Supervision, 18–19
Support networks, 104
Surgery, experimental, 83
Symptomatic presentation, 101
Syndromes, 83–84

Tarasoff, Tatiana, 104
*Tarasoff v. Regents of the University of
California*
and breach of confidentiality, 110
and dangerous client exception, 147
and dangerous clients, 70
and duty to protect or warn,
104–108
and premature release of
inpatients, 115
state statutes related to, 107, 108
Taxi Driver (film), 107
Termination of treatment, 48–51
client's right to determine, 56
sexual involvement after, 121
Test data, 69–70
Testimonial privilege

About the Authors

David L. Shapiro, PhD, is a professor of psychology at Nova Southeastern University in Fort Lauderdale, Florida, where he teaches courses in ethics and professional issues, forensic assessment, criminal law, consultation and supervision, and projective testing. He was formerly an associate professor of psychology at the John Jay College of Criminal Justice in New York. Dr. Shapiro has also taught many continuing education seminars for state and national psychological associations in the areas of professional liability and malpractice. He is the author of numerous books and articles, all having to do with the interface of psychology and law. He has served on the Ethics Committee of the American Psychological Association and has chaired the Ethics Committee of the American Board of Professional Psychology. He is currently president of Division 46 (Media Psychology) of the American Psychological Association. He is a diplomate of the American Board of Professional Psychology (forensic) and has served as an examiner for that board. He has been involved in the practice and teaching of forensic psychology for over 40 years.

Steven R. Smith, MA, JD, is president, dean, and professor of law at California Western School of Law in San Diego. He has lectured and written widely in the areas of mental health law and law and medicine. Areas of special interest include confidentiality and privilege, malpractice, the mental health care delivery system, and expert witnesses. In addition to being active in legal education, he has served as the public member of several mental health organizations, including the American Psychological Association Ethics Committee and the boards of the National Register and the American Board of Professional Psychology. He also is a founding member of the board of the Association for the Accreditation of Human Research Protection Programs. His MA (economics) and JD degrees are from the University of Iowa. Previously he taught at the University of Louisville and Cleveland State University. He has received a variety of awards for creative teaching, research and scholarship, and outstanding service.